What Christian leaders are saying about . . .

Pray Naked: Ten Secrets to a Sizzling Marriage

"In their book, *Pray Naked: Ten Secrets to a Sizzling Marriage,* Steve and Pam Bond let us peek inside their relationship to discover the joy, passion, and pleasure that's possible with a Christ-centered marriage. *Pray Naked* is real, it's helpful, and it's fun!"

Dr. Kevin Leman, New York Times Bestselling Author of *Have a New Sex Life by Friday* **and** *The Birth Order Book*

"Who can resist a title like this? Many husbands may be thinking 'Yes!' while many wives may be thinking, 'Um, no!' But I encourage you to read this book together with an open heart. Steve and Pam Bond have many unique insights and encouraging things to say about how couples can forge deeper avenues of intimacy in their marriage. *Pray Naked* will challenge you, encourage you, and help you draw spiritually, emotionally, and yes, physically closer to your spouse. Reading this book will benefit your relationship!"

Dr. Greg Smalley
Vice President, Marriage and Family Formation
Focus on the Family

"For a long time I have been looking for a book about marriage that is BOTH honest and hopeful! Well, here it is. *Pray Naked: Ten Secrets to a Sizzling Marriage* is raw and refreshing. Steve and Pam Bond have courageously 'pulled back the curtain' in their own marriage to show us how to warm up a cold relationship. This is one of the most vulnerable and honest books I've ever read! Get it. Read it. And pass it on!"

Ray Johnston, Senior Pastor
Bayside Church, Granite Bay, California

"I admit that I was not a fan of receiving another book on marriage, even if it was from a good friend of mine. However, I soon realized that this was not another marriage book, but an explicit 'how to' book on intimacy, the fuel that keeps the marriage fires going. I don't know what the Motion Picture Association would rate this book, but then again it's not for kids, it's for the parents that realize their marriage is the greatest gift they can give their kids. Steve and Pam hit this one out of the park!"

Chris Brown, Senior Pastor
North Coast Church, Vista, California

"The title of the book is shocking. And so is the content! It is amazing how shocking it is to modern ears to hear that marriage and spiritual life actually go together. I believe this book could not only start a revolution in the home, but could reconnect the bond between marriage and spirituality in a powerful way. Read it and practice what this book says!"

Dr. John Jackson
President of William Jessup University
Author & Speaker on Leadership and
Cultural Transformation

"Steve and Pam Bond go beyond typical marriage theory books and share what a husband and wife both need to hear. The Bonds had me engaged from the word 'Naked.' Finally, a pastor and wife willing to take a risk and be authentic, honest, and creative about marriage. I can't wait to plan a time away with my wife to pray naked!

Pray Naked. Who thought two words used together could bring so much richness, meaning, and life to a marriage. Steve and Pam have not been afraid to say what needs to be said when it comes to having a vibrant marriage."

Tim Winters, Executive Pastor
Shepherd Church, Porter Ranch, California

"Steve and Pam Bond have earned the right to speak. They are living what they are teaching - and this book is full of helpful, insightful, and practical help for every marriage. Their courageous honesty takes the sound principles of Scripture into the everyday reality with their specific application. This book will give your marriage hope and a vision that your marriage can thrive."

Kevin Odor, Senior Pastor
Canyon Ridge Christian Church, Las Vegas, Nevada

"This book is forged out of Steve and Pam's lasting marriage. It is honest, powerful, grounded in truth, and relevant. I highly recommend it."

Dan Frank, Senior Pastor
Grace Church, Reno, Nevada

"*Pray Naked* will have you laughing one minute and challenged the next because it hits so close to home. Steve and Pam share from their own personal experience these secrets of marriage that they have discovered and taught for many years. These principles have the potential to transform your marriage if you will put them into practice."

Shane Philip, Senior Pastor
The Crossing Church, Las Vegas, Nevada

"I've had the pleasure of having Steve and Pam as friends for over 10 years. They write like they live - with warmth, love, and passion. They're passionate about Christ and each other and it shows in what they have written in *Pray Naked*. Read this book and their passion just may rub off on you and your marriage too! They write of a lived reality and their desire is to share it and see it multiply. Get yourself a copy. Read it! Enjoy it! Grow!"

Brent Brooks, Senior Pastor
Reno Christian Fellowship, Reno, Nevada.

Pray Naked

Chris,

Thanks for the terrific
endorsement!

Blessings!

Steve Brad

Eph 2:10

Pray Naked

Ten Secrets to a Sizzling Marriage

Stephen and Pamela Bond

Foreword by Gene Appel

Pray Naked: Ten Secrets to a Sizzling Marriage
Copyright © 2017 by Stephen and Pamela Bond
All Rights Reserved

ISBN 978-1-7321457-1-9 (International Trade Paper Edition)

First Printing
June 2018

Editor
TJ Martini

Layout and Design
Gary Lebeck

Cover Design
Myranda Rogers

Back Cover Photograph
Emily Loftus

Publisher
Living Well Ministries LLC

Scripture quotations marked (NIV) are taken from the Holy Bible, New International Version®, NIV®. Copyright © 1973, 1978, 1984, 2011 by Biblica, Inc.™ Used by permission of Zondervan. All rights reserved worldwide. www.zondervan.com The "NIV" and "New International Version" are trademarks registered in the United States Patent and Trademark Office by Biblica, Inc.™

Printed in the United States of America
14 13 12 11 10 / RMG / 10 9 8 7 6 5 4 3 2 1

Dedication

This book is dedicated to our four amazing children: Rachel, Christina, Jennifer, and Tommy, for without you, our story would not be complete; our hearts would not be as full; our lives would not be as blessed.

For many years, we have pondered sharing with you these marriage secrets, waiting until the time was right. You are all adults now. Yet we still ask ourselves, what can we give you at this point in your lives that would make a difference to your future? What more can we offer? What lessons can we share?

We know that we have made mistakes, not only as your parents but also as a married couple. We are quite certain that through your eyes our marriage looks completely different than it does from ours.

Still, with everything we have been through together, our greatest hope is that you have been able to see how much we truly love Jesus, that we are still madly in love with each other and that we sincerely want to accomplish God's plan that he has set before us.

This book is about marriage and what we have learned throughout this magnificent journey together. We want you to know that marriage is a gift from God, and although no marriage is perfect, it can, with hard work and God's grace, bring the most incredible joy and satisfaction.

We love you very much,
Dad and Mom

PRAY NAKED

Ten Secrets to a Sizzling Marriage

Stephen and Pamela Bond

Foreword by Gene Appel

Artist Myranda Rogers
Cover oil painting explanation:

"After reading two chapters of the book, I did a painting in response. This cover features that original artwork done in oil on canvas. Pam's description of 'perfect peace' while laying in the arms of her husband was beautiful enough to be the very cover of the book!"

Table of Contents

Acknowledgements

Above all, we thank God for the privilege he's given us over the past 40+ years to experience his lavish love, for the honor of serving him in various locations around the globe, and for his amazing gift of marriage.

We also thank our incredible spiritual family, including our second-to-none staff and elders at Summit Christian Church, for continuing to dream with us for the past two decades and for allowing us the time and bandwidth to write this book.

We are also eternally grateful to the leadership of our home church, Eastside Christian Church in Southern California, for launching us into ministry many years ago and then teaching us about grace when we needed it most.

Over the years we have seen scores of flourishing

examples of vibrant Christ-centered marriages. Each of these couples taught us invaluable lessons that have borne fruit in our own marriage. This book is a compilation of the wisdom and grace these precious couples have poured into us.

Special thanks to Patti Edwards (and her late husband Ed) for generously allowing us to use their home in Long Boat Key, Florida as a writing haven. The beautiful sunsets along the Gulf Coast inspired much of what we have written.

We also thank the husband and wife team of Gary Lebeck and Toni (TJ) Martini. Without their persistent encouragement, prayers and cheerleading this book would not exist.

Foreword

I grew up about 30 miles from Normal, Illinois, and there's another town downstate called Oblong, Illinois. There was a marriage one time between two people from those two towns, and when the local newspaper printed the marriage announcement the heading read: Oblong man marries Normal woman.

It's always exciting to watch two people fall in love and overdose on romance. We've all witnessed eager brides and grooms walk down the aisle and light the unity candle by merging their individual candle flames into one. At this point they believe this will be the metaphor for their marriage. They are headed toward a marriage that sizzles. They dream that their marriage will experience nothing by happy, happy, happy...and bliss, bliss, bliss! But a short time later, well about two days later, reality sets in and they wonder why can't this person be normal like me? And they discover marriage is harder and more work than they ever dreamed. And the flame that once sizzled feels little more than a flicker.

Perhaps some of the most accurate words ever written about marriage are right out of the Bible in Ephesians 5 when the apostle Paul is discussing the relationship between a husband and wife and he notes in verse 32, *"This is a profound mystery."* Amen to that! I can't tell you how many days I have gone to bed frustrated, confused, uncertain and even bewildered by my own marriage saying, "This is a profound mystery!"

Which is why I'm so thankful my friends Steve and Pam Bond have written this book. In fact, you hold in your hands the marriage book you never thought would be written.

Let's face it, most books we've ever read on marriage, while helpful in many ways, have left us feeling like they were incomplete. It's as if the authors were holding back, unwilling to completely disclose the good, the bad, and the ugly. I think all of us have been waiting for the book that bares it all, puts it all on the table, says the last 10%, and leaves no holes barred. Finally, we have the book. *Pray Naked: Ten Secrets to a Sizzling Marriage* boldly goes where no other Christian marriage book has gone before.

Written with unusual candor, Steve and Pam dare to say the things many authors would be afraid to say, in fact things neither of them have ever put in word or print before. This is not the type of book that could be written by starry-eyed newlyweds or anybody married less than 40 years for that matter. These are the secrets to a sizzling marriage discovered and experienced by two sincere followers of Jesus in the real life ups and downs, highs and lows, the best of times and the worst of times, through their mistakes and their greatest triumphs. They reveal their sometimes painful and often fun journey to discover day to day, soul to soul, and body to body intimacy.

Over the past 10 years I've had the privilege to get an up close and personal look at Steve and Pam's life and marriage through the dynamic Summit Christian Church that they founded and lead in Sparks, Nevada. Outside of the church I serve, I have spoken more frequently and more often at Summit than anywhere else in the last decade. I've seen with my own eyes the fruit of their lives, marriage, family, and ministry. I've watched the tender and pastoral care they have for their staff, their church, their community and all the marriages and families within the span of their care. And here's what I know, they are the real deal. This book is the real deal. And you will not only find it personally transformational and helpful, but you will want to share it with every couple you know.

Gene Appel, Senior Pastor
Eastside Christian Church
Anaheim, California

Introduction

While they were still students in college, Steve and Pam met on Valentine's weekend while washing dishes at a junior high retreat sponsored by their local church. Steve was a brand new believer—just three months earlier he had accepted Christ. His world was radically turned upside down when, as a budding Marxist, Steve did an about-face to become a fire-breathing Jesus-follower. Pam came to Christ several years earlier as she moved away from traditional religiosity into a passionate life-giving relationship with Jesus. Their relationship deepened over the ensuing 18 months, and they fell deeply in love, and on August 27, 1977, the two became husband and wife. Today, they are still head-over-heels in love.

The Bonds have been in vocational ministry throughout

their entire marriage where they have served churches in Illinois, Wisconsin, and Nevada. They were also missionaries in Chile, South America for ten years.

In 1999, they planted Summit Christian Church in Sparks, Nevada. By God's grace, Summit has grown to become one of the largest churches in Northern Nevada.

Steve and Pam have four grown children and nine totally awesome grandchildren currently scattered around the globe. The two of them enjoy their family, as well as traveling, reading books out loud to one another, dreaming, and ministering to others together, especially in the area of strengthening marriages. One of the great joys in their lives is helping people experience the more and better life offered by Jesus.

Pam attended Pacific Christian College (now called Hope International University). She is passionate about ministering to women, and is hands-on involved with the Women's Encounter Ministry at Summit Church.

Steve received a Master of Divinity from Trinity Evangelical Divinity School, Deerfield IL, a Master of Theology from Fuller Theological Seminary, Pasadena, CA and a Doctor of Ministry from Gordon-Conwell Theological Seminary, South Hamilton, MA. Steve is also an avid swimmer who enjoys new challenges. Since 2004 he has competed annually in the Donner Lake Open Water Swim Race in Truckee, California. In 2017 he climbed Mount Kilimanjaro in Africa.

Throughout this book, Steve and Pam will share the secrets they have discovered to a marriage that sizzles in the fullest sense. After more than 40 years together, they still enjoy an intimate friendship. They also have a mutual commitment to serve and to pour out their lives for the benefit of other people.

Chapter One

Secret #1
Put Christ First

Steve—Pam and I are about to share with you the secrets we have discovered to a marriage that sizzles. We mean this in the fullest sense. After four decades of marriage, Pam and I enjoy an intimate friendship with each other. We have a deep and warm connection…soul to soul. We also have a passionate mutual commitment to serve others. And we enjoy fabulous and frequent celebrations of the "act of marriage." In the following pages, we will unpack the secrets we have discovered about all of these marriage blessings and more.

But it all begins with a Jesus-centered life. Nothing in this book will make any sense without an unyielding and wholehearted commitment to Christ by both the husband and wife. We can summarize everything we've learned over the years in this one statement: the closer each of us has grown to Jesus the closer we have grown to one another.

Years ago Pam and I were taught that marriage could be described as a triangle. Jesus is at the apex on top, and the husband and wife are at either point on the bottom. With this image in mind, the closer each spouse grows toward Jesus, the closer they become with each other. Pam and I have repeatedly

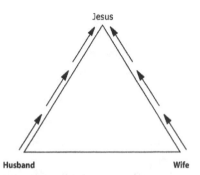

discovered this to be true. This is why before we talk about having lingering soul-bearing conversations and off-the-charts sex, we must first talk about developing a life fully centered on Jesus.

The Jesus-centered life is not a dream. It is not for the exceptional super-spiritual few. The Jesus-centered life is how the Lord envisioned everyone who followed him would live. Years ago author Watchman Nee described this as "the normal Christian life."

Jesus put it like this:

> *"Remain in me as I also remain in you. No branch can bear fruit by itself. It must remain in the vine. Neither can you bear fruit unless you remain in me. I am the vine, you are the branches. If you remain in me and I in you, you will bear much fruit. Apart from me you can do nothing"* (John 15:4-5).

To remain in Jesus is to live with a constant awareness of his presence and leaning into his power and direction. This is how Jesus calls all of his followers to live. Again, this is not only for the deeply committed...this is how Jesus expects every Christ follower to live. His calling is clear: *"Remain in me as I also remain in you."* This means living 24-7 fully aware of his presence and fully alive to his life within us.

To our great loss, we live in an age where the Christian experience is often reduced to a mere prayer when someone "crosses the line of faith." But "crossing the line of faith" is only the very beginning of a lifelong journey which ultimately consumes the entire life of the Christ follower.

Thus, as a precursor to experiencing God's fullest and richest blessing in marriage, both husband and wife must increasingly live a Christ-centered life. Remember the triangle with Jesus at the apex. The closer both the husband and wife draw toward Jesus the closer they become to one another.

One of the best descriptions in the Bible of a Jesus-centered life is found in Galatians 5:22-23. *"But the fruit of the Spirit is love, joy, peace, patience, kindness, goodness, faithfulness, gentleness, and self-control."* It's easy to see how a life filled with this rich spiritual fruit would also be fertile soil for an incredible marriage. But this begs the question: how do we cultivate a Jesus-centered life? Where do we begin?

I'm sure there are many answers to this question. But one thing is certain: we will never move toward a more fully Jesus-centered life unless we intentionally desire it. When Pam and I first became believers we jumped with both feet into our new life with Christ. Whatever "an average Christian life was" we did not want anything to do with that! This headlong desire to be fully yielded to Jesus has resulted in our lifelong pursuit of his will. Some seasons have been more fruitful than others. But again and again, we've kept coming back to wanting more of his life, his will and his control, and less of our will and less of our life in the flesh.

Nothing we have done to cultivate Christ as our center is new or remarkable. But for over forty years we have practiced the same life-giving spiritual disciplines that have nurtured Christ followers throughout the ages:

- We consistently read the Scriptures and make notes.
- We consistently spend time in prayer.
- We consistently worship and serve in a local church.
- We consistently connect to Christian community.
- We consistently give generously to the cause of Christ.

- We consistently fast.
- We consistently draw aside for times of deeper reflection.

Each of these disciplines can be practiced with rote mindlessness resulting in little life-giving value. Or they can also be platforms for genuinely connecting with Jesus. For example, reading Scripture can be a toilsome exercise to check off a "to-do" list, or it can be an opportunity to hear a fresh word from the Living Lord. The choice is ours.

But, throughout church history, those who have walked closest with Jesus have invariably practiced these basic spiritual disciples. Pam and I have too...and they have enriched us and helped us to live increasingly Jesus-centered lives.

Once again, living a Jesus-centered life is the beginning point for everything we will share about a marriage that sizzles. As a husband and wife grow closer to Jesus, they will also grow closer to each other. And the results are amazing!

Pam—Marriage is a miracle. Think about it. The husband and wife come from two different backgrounds, two different homes, with different values, priorities, and ways of communicating. Brides and grooms, starry-eyed and ignorant, go into a marriage after all the fun of preparing for the wedding. Playing house is fun but then reality hits!

Reality hit Steve and me a few weeks into our marriage, right after I had cleaned our new apartment for the first time. My new husband must not have thought I had done a very good job because (believe it or not) he re-cleaned it right after I had finished. To him, it wasn't clean enough! I was more than just upset. I was extremely hurt. And that was not the only reality check I discovered.

Before we were married, I sewed often and enjoyed making things with my hands. For me, it was relaxing, and I thoroughly enjoyed it. I assumed that I would be able to continue my sewing without creating any friction. However, this assumption only lasted a couple of weeks when Steve was walking through the apartment barefoot and stepped on a straight pin that had fallen into the carpet. Ouch! The reality of our marriage honeymoon once again began to fade.

Shopping also became a reality check for us every time I went to the store. I learned quickly that Steve wanted brand name items in the refrigerator...different brand names than those I had been brought up with.

The truth was that Steve had his own ideas of what married life would look like because of his upbringing. And I had my set of expectations, some of which were realistic, but many of which were very naive.

God apparently knew that our marriage was going to need extra help. While Steve was in the Munich Airport awaiting my flight to see him the Christmas before we were married, he met a Christian counselor whose office was an hour away from our home in California. The two of them struck up a conversation which resulted in an offer of free pre-marital counseling when we returned to the USA. Did I say FREE? Yes! I don't know what got into the counselor, other than the Holy Spirit saying, "Look, these two are going to need some major help!"

Six weeks before we tied the knot, we drove the hour to Pasadena, California and had our first session. I will never forget how the counselor bent down next to me and verbalized what I was thinking, but not able to say. Then he did the same for Steve. He must have been thinking, "Sheesh! Lord, help these people!"

An issue surfaced when the counselor asked Steve to visualize a day in the life of the new Bond household. My husband-to-be started out describing his image of our new early morning routine, as he envisioned it. All was fine until he said he was going to read the newspaper while he ate breakfast. I immediately said, "Wait! You can't do that! You have to talk to me when you eat breakfast!"

In my family of origin, we were not allowed to even read the back of a cereal box at the breakfast table because we talked together. Hmmm. Not a good sign. (The humorous part of this is for most of our marriage we never had enough money to purchase the daily newspaper even if we had wanted it.)

After our first session, we were given homework to fill out a comprehensive psychological assessment, and the counselor would review the results with us later. On the way home from the appointment, Steve and I got into a huge fight. I don't remember if it had to do with reading the newspaper at the breakfast table or not. But, in any case, we decided to go directly to Denny's Restaurant to fill out our psychological assessments so we could send them in.

Steve got a call a week later from the counselor asking about the circumstances surrounding us as we took the test. Evidently, Steve's results were fine, but my results indicated that I was psycho! The counselor realized that the results of the test were not in agreement with who he had experienced.

But, looking back, the test may have been more right than he realized. I was a very tightly wound young woman with definite feelings that were much too fragile.

I can speak from experience today that any marriage that succeeds is a miracle. In the following pages, I will share how Steve and I had to learn how to communicate. Though we had a lot to learn, we were a miracle in the making. How did we survive? Well, I would say, we both loved Jesus so much that when we were at odds with each other, we would run (or sometimes crawl) to him. Maybe not the first day or two, but eventually, when we finally got over being so stinking mad, we turned to God and asked for his help.

The first years our disagreements were full of the "silent treatment." I would be so angry I would cry. Steve would retreat because he didn't know what to do and needed to calm down. After a day or two, he had worked through things in his own mind and was thinking that things were back to normal...and that I had reached the same place. But I was still struggling, and the anger had turned to hurt. As a result, every time we were at odds it took a long time to get back on an even keel.

Over the years we have learned to voice our feelings and work through our differences more effectively. Those silent days have grown fewer, but we still annoy each other at times and continue to have our moments of selfishness and pride. But we have increasingly learned to run to the Lord when we are aware of our sin. We confess and receive his forgiveness. The more often we have done this, the easier it has become.

This is why Steve and I are convinced that God's ideal design for marriage begins with both husband and wife seeking God first. When both are living a Christ-centered life, it results in the married couple knowing and trusting God more and more which draws them closer and closer together.

Steve—As we go through the following pages, we will often discuss how to experience a sizzling marriage. Pam and I are occasionally asked by couples how this can become a reality in their marriage. To the husband, we would say, "It starts with you, but not only you."

Men are instructed in Scripture to love their wives as Christ loves the church and gave himself up for her. When a husband does this, he will consider his wife his first ministry. He will love his wife unconditionally, unreservedly and unabashedly. He will look for ways to serve her, to show her his love and concern, and create a safe place for her to grow to become all that she can be. When a husband loves his wife as Christ loves the church, he cares for her and pays attention to her feelings, desires, and needs. He creates a safe place for her to grow in beauty.

Husbands, if you don't know where to begin, then start with this prayer. "God, help me to love my wife as you love the church. Please show me how to do this! I want to serve her; I want to die to myself for her. Lord, help me listen to her and know her heart, even if my needs are not being met right away."

Did you just pray that? If you did, then trust that God will hear your prayer and show you what your wife needs. Remember that a wife usually responds to her husband's love. If she feels loved by you and feels heard and taken into account; if she feels more important than your job, your parents and your friends, then you are well on your way to becoming a very happy husband. It may take time. There may be old habits to overcome and dance steps which have made deep ruts in your living room carpet that need to be relearned. But, in time, God can work miracles!

Husbands, after you pray for God to show you how to love your wife as Christ loves the church, then, ask her how she feels loved. "Honey, what do I do that makes you feel loved?" What says "I love you" to one wife, may not say it to another. Ask your bride questions. Get to know her. Listen to her. Ask her advice. Date her. Spend time and money on her. Invest in her. Put aside what you want to do and do whatever would make her feel loved.

Pam—Now, to the wife who desires greater sizzle with her husband, Steve and I would also say, "It starts with you, but not only you." There has been a huge backlash over the last 50 years as women have rebelled against the picture of the wife, in her apron, doing everything for her demanding husband. Young wives have told me they refuse to get their husband a glass of water if he can do it himself. They say they don't want to be his "slave." This saddens me, but quite honestly, I have seen unhealthy marriages where the husband is so demanding that he expects his wife to wait on him hand and foot.

However, wives, our human nature is quick to say, "When he starts loving me like Christ loves the church, then I'll start doing my part." But someone has to take the first step. Ask God to help you minister to your husband, pray for him, serve him, look for ways to outdo him in your attempt to show your love and tenderness.

The bottom line is this: men want to be respected. Wives can demean their husband and not even be aware that they are disrespecting him. Someone once said that behind a great man is often an even greater woman. Wives need to know what power they have to help their husband to become great!

So, wives, "It starts with you, but not only you." Pray that God would help you respect and treat your husband with kindness. Remember that we are called to first respect our husband and then, secondly, to train our children. Not the other way around.

Reach out and ask God to help you, then go to your husband and ask him how you can make him feel more loved. Be prepared that he will probably say he wants more sex. But, please understand that for a husband, sex is one of the tangible ways a wife can show her husband that she truly loves him and wants to minister to him. He will probably be more willing to open up about other areas of his life, once he feels listened to and after his needs are taken into account. Be patient.

Sizzle in marriage will only happen when the marriage relationship is made a priority, an investment, something worth working on in the good times and the bad times.

Thus, when we say, "It starts with you, but not only you," it means both husband and wife committing to doing their best by yielding themselves completely to Jesus.

The Bible teaches us to submit one to another as we submit ourselves to the Lord. This deference goes against our human nature, but the dividends are breathtaking. Stumbling will happen, but as we give grace to one another, and with God's Spirit to guide and strengthen, sizzle will come.

Steve—So, there is secret #1, which is not really a secret, but it does go counter to our human nature. My human nature wants life to be all about me, my wants, my desires, my timetable and my way. It is not a secret because it is right there in God's word for all to read. We just have to pick it up and read what it says—and then do it.

Our prayer is that you find the sizzle in your marriage that you were meant to have. It will take years and a great deal of hard work. It will take denying yourself and seeking the Lord with all of your heart. It will take the work of the Holy Spirit of God. But it will be one of the most rewarding things you will ever encounter on this earth.

Pam and I started this book years ago as a compilation

of our life experiences to give to our four adult children. However, in the ensuing years, as we grew in our personal understanding of marriage, we began sensing God's direction to share these ideas with our church family. We are now "mom and dad" and "grandma and grandpa" not only to our biological family but also (in a manner of speaking), to a large congregation of spiritual children, whom we love dearly.

The needs are clear. One of the most frequent prayer requests in our home church is pleading for God's help with struggling marriages. Our desire is that God would be glorified throughout these pages and that marriages would be strengthened. And it begins in our spiritual lives because the first secret to a marriage that sizzles is putting Christ first.

Chapter Two

Secret #2

Become Best Friends

P am—I was scheduled to be a volunteer student coach at our church's junior high winter retreat in the mountains in Southern California near Lake Arrowhead. For the previous year, I had been teaching the 8th-grade girl's Sunday School Class at Eastside Christian Church. I was nineteen years old at the time, and I thoroughly enjoyed my growing relationships with these girls. So I knew the upcoming retreat was going to be a blast!

Just before we left, I was introduced to a handsome young man named Steve who was also going on the retreat as a coach. I soon learned that he was the same Steve who we had been in prayer for at the request of my friend Ron. Ron was the president of the college group at church, and he would come to our gatherings to report how his roommate (Steve) was asking questions about God. The two of them had been staying up late at night debating various theological issues. Not too long after, Ron shared with us that God had answered our prayers and that Steve had finally accepted Christ as his Savior. To my surprise and delight, this same Steve was now going on the junior high retreat.

The weekend of the retreat was snowy, with students racing down the hillsides on inner tubes. I came inside to get warm and noticed Steve standing by the fire. Shortly after, one of the junior high girls approached him and asked if he would go back outside and race down the hill with her group again. Steve didn't hesitate for a minute. He quickly left the warmth of the fire and went into another room to put back on his cold, wet clothes, then out again he went in the snow to be with the kids. It was at this time that I first noticed his servant's heart.

The family that arranged for us to use their cabin also planned the meals. One meal was split pea soup. Another was onion soup. Can you imagine serving those things to junior high students? Not surprisingly, there were a lot of leftovers! After each meal, I went to the kitchen to help, and I noticed Steve was already there washing dishes at every opportunity. Hmmm. Not very typical for a 21-year-old guy! It was during this time when he was at the sink that I got to know Steve. He was funny, thoughtful, kind, and did I say handsome? I came home from the retreat completely "ga-ga" over this new friend and patiently waited for him to call me. It took him a month to finally ask me out on our first date.

Friendship is another secret to experiencing a marriage that sizzles. Truth be told, Steve and I were extremely good friends from the beginning. We quickly went from washing dishes together on the junior high retreat to traveling down to Tijuana, Mexico on the weekends to serve orphans.

But our friendship had a long way to grow to become all that God intended. Steve was hard driving with visions, goals, and dreams. He wanted to change the world for the cause of Christ! I've said for decades that Steve lives two years ahead of everyone else. He has this knack for seeing the great things God could do if people would pull together.

Another word for this is visionary. Yes, Steve has always been a visionary. I, on the other hand, used to be more of a homebody. I would have been content to stay home and sew, do crafts and make my home a lovely place to live. But that's not who God wanted me to be! So, the Lord yoked me up with Steve in order to help unleash my own leadership gifts. Today we are both strong leaders. We don't always agree, but over the years we have learned how to communicate our dreams, visions, passions, and desires in ways that encourage each other and work together rather than pulling in opposite directions. But for many years this was not the case.

Our first experience in a canoe showcased this. Many years ago, our entire family attended a camp in Northern Wisconsin. When we arrived, we were informed that all the married couples had to experience something they called the "Midnight Delight." After all four of our kids were safe and asleep in our cabin, Steve and I left at midnight and met up with several other couples at the dock where canoes for each of the couples were waiting. We were then given instructions to paddle our canoe toward a light in the distance. This light turned out to be a bonfire on an island, and we could see it from where we were. The camp staff told us that they would be waiting there with a surprise.

The Bond canoe wasted no time taking off, needing, of course, to be the first to make it to the island, because that's what Bonds do! But soon we found ourselves zig-zagging across the lake and floundering in the tall reeds. Can you hear the conversation? "Okay, we can do this! Back up, now, go this way! No, this way!" Our vision of being first to arrive on the island slowly dwindled.

All the other canoes arrived at the bonfire long before we did, and they had already received and eaten their s'mores surprise, while Steve and I continued to struggle to get our canoe going straight. Finally, I heard my husband's stern voice coming from the back of the canoe, "Pam, put the paddle down." I was confused. "But..." I said. "Pam, just put the paddle down!" he repeated in a much louder voice. And so I did, and the "Midnight Delight" turned into the "Midnight Fight" followed by total silence.

By the time we got to the bonfire we didn't even want the s'mores...which was a good thing as they had already been devoured. In fact, we had been on the island no more than a few minutes before the other happy couples started heading back, starry-eyed and totally in love from their romantic evening. Our not-so-positive experience in the canoe was a mirror of how, in the early years of marriage, our friendship often struggled.

Our pattern for many years was usually both of us trying to do everything ourselves in our own way. When we got frustrated with each other, we often wouldn't communicate for several hours—sometimes even days. It was hard for me as a young bride to verbalize my feelings. To help overcome this, in our first few years we would go for long walks because

I could talk as long as I didn't look at Steve's face. I think I was slightly intimidated though I eventually got over that. However, it took many more years until our communication became as open as it is today.

Steve came from a family that rarely talked about anything negative and, as a result, conflict solving was never taught. In my case, I ran from any kind of confrontation, which I usually did by acquiescing. To make matters worse, I was taught in church and in books on marriage that I was to submit to my husband...no matter what. I honestly believed that if I submitted like Sarah had done when Abraham gave her into another man's arms on TWO separate occasions (because he was afraid for his own life) that God would take care of me just like he did with Sarah.

Now, to be clear, I do believe in biblical submission of a wife to her husband. Nonetheless, I also believe the Bible when it says the wife and husband are to submit to one another! I realize there are decision-making times when the wife needs to trust her husband's judgment after her feelings, observations, and opinions have been shared. But, looking back, I think too often I replaced wholesome, biblical submission with acquiescence. Instead of voicing my opinion, to avoid conflict and sharing my ideas, I would not be completely honest with Steve and simply acquiesced much too often.

It has taken me years to learn to be more assertive and express myself. It helped a great deal when Steve learned that I feel most loved by him when he listens to me and takes what I say into account. Even if he doesn't agree with me, if I know that he has heard me and understands my concerns, if I sense that my opinion is valued and that he has my best interest in mind, then I feel loved by him. That has made a huge difference for both of us in our communication.

Communication works both ways. Just as Steve has learned to show me his love by carefully listening to me, I have also learned to communicate with him in ways that he perceives are more loving and respectful. After 40-plus years of marriage, my husband knows my heart, and so his responses are rarely defensive. If he senses something is awry in my wording he usually knows it's because there has been some misunderstanding. In other words, because he knows I love him, Steve almost always gives me the benefit of the doubt.

The Heart of Marriage Friendship

Steve—Even though Pam and I enjoy spending a considerable amount of time together, marriage friendship does not mean that a couple has to be "glued to the hip." Ideally, a husband and wife are whole persons, healthy persons, complete persons and each one brings that health into their marriage friendship. This friendship is demonstrated in many ways: trust, wanting the best for one other, doing whatever possible to help the other succeed and challenging each other to be all they can be.

I believe this is the type of friendship that describes Adam and Eve. The Bible says they were naked and not ashamed. It seems to me that Adam and Eve's marriage friendship had at least four dimensions: physical, intellectual, emotional and spiritual. All of these are important for a marriage friendship that sizzles.

Physical Friendship

Let's begin with the physical. To be genuine friends in marriage means we're not ashamed of our bodies. It means enjoying how God made each of us and that we genuinely delight in our spouse's body. (We will talk more about how much fun this can be in the chapters on Pray Naked and Have Sex Often.) Of course, this means not ridiculing one another, but looking past the imperfections and going deeper. It means that we love how God made each of us physically.

Years ago Pam worked for a cancer doctor. She remembers the doctor telling a woman with breast cancer that she needed to get her breast implants removed because they were impeding her recovery. The woman said her husband wouldn't let her do that. Apparently, the husband wanted a wife with big breasts even if it cost her life. To me, this is absurd! Our society has placed such a priority on looking perfect that we have lost sight of reality. Part of being friends in marriage is learning to love and marvel and relish in the physical body of our spouse.

For Pam and I this has resulted in our spending ample time naked together. Several years ago we stopped wearing anything to bed. We enjoy looking at each other and having our skin touch during the night, even if nothing else happens. I think that God had something extraordinary in mind for marriage when the Bible says that Adam and Eve were naked and they felt no shame. It's a beautiful part of friendship in marriage.

Intellectual Friendship

To be friends in a marriage with sizzle also means fully accepting your spouse's intellectual capabilities. In a healthy marriage, neither the husband nor the wife should feel devalued for having less to bring to the table when discussing issues. I have many more formal degrees than Pam. But she has experience, wisdom, spiritual insight and life lessons that make our intellectual engagement truly stimulating.

I have learned to listen to Pam, and she has also learned to glean from me. Pam reads extensively and shares with me what she is learning, and I do the same with her. We can think out loud, and we know that our marriage is a safe and healthy place to express ourselves freely.

Emotional Friendship

Emotionally, Pam and I have learned not be ashamed to share our deepest hurts, joys, wonders, fears, and desires. This would not be the case if either of us were mocked for sharing what we feel. If that ever happened, both of us would clam up tighter than a drum! But when we share our feelings and it's met with wonder, understanding, openness, and unconditional love, we then feel gloriously free to open up even more.

Pam has been extremely helpful teaching me to be more in touch with my feelings. Partly because I am male and partly because of my driven personality style, I have often not even known what my feelings are. Over the years my wife has helped to give me new vocabulary to express myself. Instead of settling for my default answer, "I'm tired," Pam asks clarifying questions. "Are you frustrated?" "Are you afraid?" "Are you angry?" Pam once downloaded an emotional vocabulary wheel to teach me new terms to express my feelings. Pam's coaching has expanded my ability to communicate emotionally with her and with others.

Strange as it may seem, I think watching Hallmark movies has also helped me to get more in touch with my emotions. As you probably know, Hallmark movies are almost always sappy stories that tug on our emotional heart-strings. I can always predict what will happen and I know the story line by heart, but I still get sucked in and cry every time. Gentlemen, you might also try it!

Pam—Since I am a verbal person, sharing our emotions as husband and wife makes me come alive. Steve knows this and loves this about me. (Maybe this is one reason we enjoy spending vacation time alone with no one else around.) I can laugh out loud, cry like a child, express what I am feeling with Steve and know that I won't be laughed at or put down. He's also open with me. Occasionally I share in marriage talks, that after many years, husbands and wives can communicate "soul to soul." This is part of what it means to be best friends in marriage. When this happens, both husband and wife are at total peace with themselves and with each other. It's a beautiful experience!

I remember a single friend of mine meeting Steve for the first time. The three of us had a pleasant conversation, and my friend commented to me later that she had never seen two people like us. She said, "It was like you were breathing for each other." I explained to her that what she saw was Jesus in us. But what she also saw was a reflection of the deep friendship that Steve and I enjoy in our marriage.

Spiritual Friendship

When Steve and I met, we both had a passion for God's plan and purpose for our individual lives. At 19 years old, I had made a list with the qualities I wanted in a husband. At the top of the list was someone who loved Jesus with all his heart. But, after completing my list, I thought to myself, "This seems pretty selfish. This is all about what I want for me." So, I turned the paper over and wrote a list of qualities that I wanted God to form in me, so I would be ready when I met this "man of my dreams."

For Steve and me, the spiritual dimension has always been a high priority in our relationship. But, as you know, time can go by, and if we are not regularly cultivating our relationship with God, we will no longer have Christ as the center of our lives. I cannot depend on Steve for me to have a fresh and growing relationship with God. I have to cultivate that myself. So, in my Bible reading and prayer time, in my study of books on Christian disciplines and life skills, I take personal responsibility for learning and growing.

Likewise, Steve feeds himself on God's Word and is growing in his own relationship with God. Then we come together and share what we are learning. We apply God's Word and encourage each other to be all that our Lord wants us to be.

One of my favorite things to do with my husband is to pray. Some years ago we got into the habit of waking up a few mornings a week, and taking turns going to the kitchen, bringing back a cup of coffee for me and orange juice for him. While still in bed, the two of us talk, have our drinks and then pray before we get up. This small act in itself has added more sizzle to our relationship that you could ever imagine!

Married Friendship is Not Exclusive

Friendship as a married couple does not have to be exclusive. I am free to have girlfriends, time alone and pursue my passions. And Steve is free to have his friends, his time alone, and pursue his dreams.

When we got married, Steve gave me a bracelet with a quote from Ecclesiastes 4:12 written on it: *"A chord of three strands is not quickly broken."* The third chord primarily represents Jesus. But it's also a reminder that a healthy marriage relationship needs to involve other people to sharpen us, to hone us and to keep us accountable. An unhealthy marriage becomes so exclusive that it keeps everyone else away. God designed us to live in community, so we have the richness of other people to interact with.

This way of life was learned early in our marriage. At the beginning of Steve's second year in seminary, I began working at the school so I could be with him more. It was an excellent opportunity for me to see the inner workings of the school and to be part of the seminary family. Steve also began serving as a Youth Pastor in a small church in

Prospect Heights, IL. We had been volunteer coaches in the junior high group in our home church in California while we dated, but this was "real ministry." Steve even got paid!

Not surprisingly, it was hard for me as a young wife to have my husband constantly at school or youth pastoring which left little time or energy for me. I remember complaining to Steve one day, and his response was, "Pam, I can't be your lady friend. You have to get out and make friends. I can't talk to you about cooking and sewing and lady stuff." This was a new concept for me. I had assumed that my husband would be my everything. Looking back, I needed Steve's encouragement to get out and have a life other than waiting for him to have time for me.

Thankfully, I made some wonderful friends in seminary. One friend in particular may have saved our marriage. Her name was Ellen. She and I were both pregnant with our first child, so we would meet before work and walk around the basketball court at the college next to the seminary. This was our only form of exercise since the winter weather in Northern Illinois was not conducive to outdoor "pregnant lady" activities.

In time, Ellen and I also swapped (or bartered) our skills. I sewed maternity clothes for her, and she typed my husband's seminary papers. She had her Master's Degree in business and was a whiz with Greek and Hebrew fonts on her IBM Selectric typewriter that made Steve's seminary papers look sharp.

I had typed Steve's papers his first year in school, and since he tends to be a perfectionist, this became a huge source of stress for us. Back before computers were available, if a typed page had too many smudges, it had to be retyped all over again. Ugh! How precious of God to bring me a wonderful friend who would bless us with her typing skills and whom I could also bless with my sewing skills. Throughout our marriage, God has continued to bring friends for both Steve and me who have enriched us separately and together. The best marriages always include a few trusted friends.

That said, it is a beautiful thing for your spouse to be your "best friend." It's incredible to be married to someone who knows you better than anyone on this earth and still loves you. True marriage friendship happens when your spouse accepts you for who you are, wants your very best, cheers you on to reach your greatest potential and would die to protect you, no matter what.

When a husband and wife enjoy married friendship, they know personal things won't be shared outside of the relationship to embarrass the spouse or paint them in a negative light. It is a relationship that can sit for hours and not say a word but still communicate total acceptance and peace. It is a depth of friendship that senses when the other is not feeling right because of a squint, a furrowed brow, or a slight dip in a tone of voice. No one else knows you quite as profoundly as this best friend—your spouse. This is God's excellent plan. The gift of marriage friendship is vital for a marriage to sizzle!

Keep Working on Your Friendship

Steve—In the film "50 First Dates," the character played by Drew Barrymore has amnesia. She wakes up every day completely unaware that she is married to the character played by Adam Sandler. So every day, Adam has to help Drew Barrymore fall back in love with him.

I think the film presents an interesting challenge. I wonder how it would affect all of our relationships if we treated people every day in a way that would cultivate their love. You know as well as I do that we can settle into routines with people and take them for granted. This can happen in any relationship, but especially in marriage.

This shows up in big and small ways. We get lazy and stop saying thank you. We forget to tell our spouse that we love them, or that we respect them, or that they're beautiful, or handsome, or that we appreciate all they do for us. So, "50 First Dates," in a sense, presents a challenge to all of us who are married. What if every day we treated our spouse like we treated them when we were dating? What if every day we made it a priority to be so kind that our spouse would fall in love with us all over again? Now that would put sizzle into a marriage!

Most couples begin their relationship as friends. Pam shared earlier that we met while serving at a junior high retreat. Afterward, we began hanging out together with a group of friends from church. We weren't dating. We were just friends. At that time, the young adults in our church often went to a restaurant called Fiddlers Three to have dessert and talk.

After a month or so, I finally asked Pam out on a date. On our first date, we went to a Christian concert on a Saturday night at the Calvary Chapel in Costa Mesa, CA. Eventually, Pam told me that she was interested in missions. That got me fired up because I was passionate about changing the world. (I was an aspiring Marxist before I became a Christian, and changing the world has always been my goal.) I used to say that I had no interest in being an "average American" living in suburbia. I was a brand-new Christian, and I wanted to charge the gates of hell with a squirt gun!

While we dated, we not only worked at an orphanage in Tijuana, Mexico, we also spent several weeks in Mexico City at another orphanage. When you see someone work hard in another culture without knowing the language, you find out quickly what they're made of.

The first time I kissed Pam was in the parking lot outside of my apartment. I think we'd been dating for about two months. Over time our friendship grew into a romantic relationship. Shortly after, I went to a Torchbearer Bible School in Holsby Brunn, Sweden for eight months. We were young and in love, and the separation was hard, but it was incredibly helpful too. It allowed our relationship to deepen through our letters back and forth. (This was long before email existed.) Since I was a new Christian, being in Sweden also allowed me time to grow in the Lord while I was 5,000 miles away from Pam. I had to lean on Jesus, which was very important in our growing relationship.

Pam—Even though Steve was in Sweden and we were "long-distant dating," I stayed busy in Bible College with my own studies and part-time employment. I was also involved in the college group at church and served in the student ministry. Writing letters allowed us time to put our thoughts and feelings down on paper and say things we may not have said at that time had we been face to face. So, we were friends first, and Christ was the center of our relationship. Then, our friendship grew into a romance, and we eventually got married being the closest of friends.

Everyone's journey is different, but what we've seen time and time again is that married couples are good friends when they first get married. But over time they stop being good friends and they start being something else. For example, we've seen couples over the years who have become more like business partners rather than close friends. Maybe they're both working super hard in their careers—and there is nothing wrong with that unless their careers end up trumping their marriage.

When this happens, all the couple talks about is their work, or their investments, or the new house they want, or the next exotic vacation they have planned. Scrape it all away, and the primary thing that holds them together is making money and spending money. When this happens, sometimes the friendship dies, and sadly they essentially become more or less business partners.

We've also seen couples who have become more like child-care providers than good friends. This happens when the kids eat up every ounce of time and energy, so mom and dad have nothing left to give to each other.

In our case, there have been times when Steve and I have become ministry machines, and all we did was produce for the ministry. During those seasons, all of our energy went into ministry, and that was all we talked about. During those occasions, there's no way we would have said we were primarily best friends; teammates maybe, ministry machines for sure, but not close friends at all.

In contrast, I love how the wife describes her husband in Song of Songs. Song of Songs is, of course, the most romantic book in the Bible. It tells a passionate love story between a husband and wife. At one point the wife says: *"This is my beloved, this is my friend"* (Song of Songs 5:16). Steve and I can testify that during the past 40 years, the seasons when we've been extremely close friends have been the sweetest seasons in our marriage. Friendship makes a huge difference, and it sure makes a marriage sizzle!

Common Interests

Steve—I hope you can see how vital friendship is for a sizzling marriage. These are some of the practical ways that Pam and I express our friendship:

• We call or text each other during the day to see how we're doing.

• Pam buys me the brand-name foods that I like, and I occasionally surprise her with flowers or treats.

• Pam does the cooking, and I do the dishes. We enjoy working in the kitchen as a team every night when we're home for dinner.

• When I need a sack lunch, Pam puts love notes in with the food.

• I will surprise Pam by washing her car.

• Even though it's not her favorite thing to do, Pam goes on hikes with me.

Those are just a few examples of what it means for us to be close friends. Now, I don't know who comes to mind when you think of your childhood "best friend," or what that friendship looked like for you, but sharing common interests probably played a significant role. It certainly does in marriage friendship. This means you share some important things in common, which is more than merely sharing the same address or the same last name. We've all known couples who shared the same address, but they had practically nothing else in common. But real friends, the kind of close friends we love and cherish, share things in common.

We mentioned earlier that most couples begin their marriage as friends and they usually share some common interests. But sometimes, over time, they have less and less in common, which is why some married people stop being close friends and turn into primarily business partners or child care providers or, in our case, occasionally into ministry machines.

P am—Now, I want to be clear that I don't expect Steve to be my best "girl-friend." I don't even try to involve him in a conversation about recipes, make-up or fashion. That would be ridiculous! Steve also doesn't expect me to be a "guy friend" either.

What we are talking about is developing common interests that we both share so we can enjoy being together. If there is something that one of us does not like doing, then the one who likes it can say, "That's okay, we don't have to do that together. Let's look for something we both enjoy."

For example, I came to a point where my years of backpacking had come to an end. I was no longer enjoying it. Earlier in our marriage, I enjoyed this outdoor experience, and we created some great family memories doing it. But on the last trip Steve and I took alone, I decided it wasn't fun for me anymore. I appreciate that my husband hasn't pushed me on it, even though he probably would still like me to go backpacking with him every once in a while. However, we only have a few precious weekends a year to get away, and we'd rather spend them together doing things we both enjoy than going our separate ways.

Friendship is about "give and take." I don't like "action-bloody-cut-off-the-head" movies. Steve knows they make me physically ill. So, if he wants me to watch a movie with him, he doesn't ask me to watch action films. Instead, he'll let me choose a chick-flick. Now that is a friendship that sizzles! (I also have no problem with him seeing action movies with his guy friends.)

Steve is not the only one who accommodates. When we lived in Wisconsin, everyone was a Green Bay Packer fan. I decided early on that it would make Steve happy if I learned as much as I could about football so that I could watch the game and enjoy it with him. Surprisingly, as time went on, I actually started to enjoy football. Now we look forward to football season when we can watch the Packer games together.

A few years ago we were in San Francisco after Christmas for a couple of days of R&R. It was a Sunday afternoon, and after we checked into our hotel, we decided to walk the streets and find a place where we could have lunch and also watch football. At the time, the 49ers were doing well and so were the Green Bay Packers. Now, this might surprise you, but the two of us had never been in an Irish Pub before (remember Steve is a pastor). But the more we walked around, the more we began to realize that a pub was the only place other than our hotel room that we'd be able to eat and watch football.

After a while, we finally got up enough nerve and walked into a pub that was packed to the gills. Low and behold there was one tiny table left, so we sat down. What was even better was that our table was directly in front of two TV screens; one with the 49er game and one with the Packer game. We had loads of fun rooting for both teams and watching the games on side-by-side screens. It was a great memory together!

What made it so special was that we were doing something new. That's a common interest we share. We had never been in a pub before. We also enjoyed watching the games. Football is another common interest we share. Even though we were in a crowd of people, no one knew us so we could enjoy being alone with each other. We live very public lives most of the time, so we thoroughly enjoy whenever we can squirrel away time to be anonymous. That's another common interest we share.

For most of us, sharing common interests will mean give and take. We can't expect our spouse to be interested in everything we want to do because we are not going to be interested in everything they want to do. That's why it's vital to look for things that you both enjoy doing together. We only have limited amounts of time and money for discretionary activities. This means we need to be selective. Steve and I have discovered that choosing to do things that we both enjoy has grown our friendship.

As a result, we're occasionally going to have to choose not to do something we really want to do so we can share something in common with each other. This might not happen all the time. However, I guarantee it will happen some of the time. Not surprisingly, the more we choose common interests as husband and wife, the more sizzle we will have in our marriage friendship.

I realize doing things with family and friends is important. However, to become close friends as a married couple, it is vital to do some things alone. This allows you to create memories with just the two of you. Some of the most treasured memories that Steve and I have shared in the past few years are ours alone because we were alone as a couple when we made them.

I hope you can see how important friendship is in marriage. Becoming best friends with your spouse is an incredibly important secret to a sizzling marriage. Yes, it takes commitment as well as give and take to develop and maintain common interests as a couple. But it is like having money in the bank. So keep working on it!

Chapter Three

Secret #3

Selflessly Serve Each Other

Pam—A while back we were in Bolivia to visit a new church we planted with Compassion International. One night our flight had been delayed, and we got stuck in the airport in La Paz, Bolivia for about three hours. La Paz is one of the highest cities in the world with an elevation over 13,000 feet above sea level, and it was freezing. As we sat in the waiting area for our plane, it started getting even more frigid by the minute. That was when we noticed the door to go outside was stuck in the open position, making matters even worse and causing the temperature inside to drop to the same degree as the temperature outside.

Neither of us had brought our heavy coats and the longer we waited, the colder we got. We tried everything to stay warm—walking around and jumping up and down until our bodies were tired and we were out of breath. At one point, Steve wrapped his arms around me and held me close, and then he rubbed my arms and back hoping to bring me some comfort. It was at that moment I noticed my husband selflessly serving me, trying desperately to keep me warm, with no thought about himself. Selfishly serving each other is another secret to a marriage that sizzles.

Sadly, what too often happens in marriage is that husbands and wives end up living for themselves. Many people buy into the myth that real love shouldn't be a lot of work. We live in a culture that is incredibly idealistic with regard to love. Somehow this fairy tale version has become a fantasy that people actually believe can happen.

This is pointed out in Timothy Keller's book, *The Meaning of Marriage*. Keller repeats a quote he has heard countless times in his marriage counseling: "Love shouldn't be this hard; it should come naturally." Keller indicates one reason marriage love is so hard is that "marriage used to be about us, but now it's about me." There has been a considerable shift in our culture in how we think about life in general and marriage in particular. People seem to be more self-centered today about many things, including marriage.

In his book, Keller quotes legal scholar John Witte Jr., who says,

> "The earlier ideal of marriage as a permanent contractual union designed for the sake of mutual love, procreation,

and protection is slowly giving way to a new reality of marriage as a terminal sexual contract designed for the gratification of the individual parties."

So, as our culture has grown more and more self-centered, it has led to a shift in how we think about marriage. Today, for many people, it is strictly about personal satisfaction. Marriage is not about us anymore. It's all about me.

There are all kinds of problems with this thinking. But the most basic is that whenever we are self-centered, it is sin. The essence of sin is selfishness. Sin is doing things my way, not God's way. Selfishness is at the heart of sin in any area of life, including marriage. Because we are all broken people, at times we will all be selfish. This means that I am not a perfect wife and Steve is not a perfect husband. We will never be perfect until we are with the Lord in heaven. However, the more we choose to go against the grain and selflessly serve each other, the more sizzle we will experience in marriage.

The Way of Christ

Steve—One reason marriage takes so much work is that we are all broken people and self-centered by nature. This broken, self-centeredness can show up in the most ridiculous ways. The other evening, Pam poured some mixed nuts into a bowl for us to munch on as we talked about our day while dinner was cooking. I unwisely mentioned that the nuts were not the brand that I preferred. Pam got defensive and told me rather curtly that I could either eat them or have no nuts at all... because it was all we had. It was a moment of tension that snuck up on us with no warning. Neither of us were acting particularly Christ-like!

Selfishness can slip into any marriage at the drop of a hat. Sometimes we don't even realize it's happening until things have gotten out of hand. We act this way because we are broken people, and we desperately need our Savior, Jesus Christ, as the foundation of our marriage. Once Jesus invades our life, he slowly moves us away from being selfish to becoming more and more selfless. (Although the brand of nuts we prefer can become a stumbling block.) This is why we need to learn to walk in the way of Jesus so we can experience the joy of a sizzling marriage.

Scripture is clear about how we are to live. Mark 8:34 says, *"Whoever wants to be my disciple must deny themselves and take up their cross and follow me."* Self-denial and self-sacrifice are at the heart of following Christ. So when I'm following Christ, when I'm walking as a true disciple, it is not about me.

This is true for all areas of my life, but I think you can see how this entirely changes our approach to marriage. If we are following Christ and living a life of self-denial and self-sacrifice, then our marriage is not based on selfishness. It's not all about me. Instead, it's based on selflessness and serving my spouse.

The Apostle Paul writes,

> *"Do nothing out of selfish ambition or vain conceit. Rather, in humility value others above yourselves, not looking to your own interests but each of you to the interests of the others"* (Philippians 2:3-4).

Quite simply, this means thinking about others first. It means allowing others to go ahead of you in line. This enormously affects how we treat each other in marriage!

Be Filled With the Spirit

All of this brings us to Ephesians 5 which is one of the most critical passages in the Bible dealing with marriage. In chapter 5, Paul outlines a whole series of implications as we follow Christ. And before he jumps into marriage, he sets it up with verse 18. *"Do not get drunk on wine, which leads to debauchery. Instead, be filled with the Spirit."*

To be filled with the Holy Spirit means living with a constant awareness of God's presence and open to his power and guidance. God wants us to live like this 24-7. The more consistently we live a Spirit-filled life, the more Christ-like we will become and the more fruit of the Spirit we'll see in our lives. Love, joy, peace, patience, kindness, goodness, faithfulness, gentleness, and self-control will be more and more evident.

The passage on marriage in Ephesians begins with the command to *"be filled with the Spirit."* Every husband and every wife on this planet is broken. We are broken people saved by God's grace. And because we are all broken, left to ourselves, we will almost always default to being selfish. The only remedy for selfishness is for the Holy Spirit to transform us from the inside out.

Because of this, the best thing we can do for our marriage is to live a Spirit-filled life. As we focus on our part, becoming the kind of Spirit-filled, fruit-bearing spouse God wants us to become, many of the issues we struggle with in marriage might just work themselves out. For example, heated words and arguing would be replaced with thankfulness and joy.

And this thankfulness and joy aren't artificially manufactured. The transformation is genuine, and it happens as we learn to be filled with the Holy Spirit daily. This is why being filled with the Spirit is essential to living a life of selflessness. This is vital because selflessly serving each other is one of the secrets to a marriage that sizzles.

Submit to One Another

Pam—Paul goes on in Ephesians 5:21. *"Submit to one another out of reverence for Christ."* Submission is a foul word for many people in our culture. Once again, this is because the world screams at us that we need to take care of ourselves first and we deserve this, that, or the other thing.

But to follow Jesus means putting him and his kingdom first. Jesus said, *"But seek first his kingdom and his righteousness and all these things will be given to you as well"* (Matthew 6:33). Following Jesus means putting him first and if we do this, then we will also *"serve one another humbly in love"* (Galatians 5:13).

The surprising thing is that when we live this way, and we put God first, we end up gaining everything. It's counter-intuitive. The more we press to be first, the more we clamor for our rights, the less fulfilling life is. But the more we yield ourselves to God and serve others, the more satisfying life becomes. This is especially true in marriage.

Our family has chuckled for years about what a neat-freak Steve is. He's been that way his entire life, and when we first got married, his neat-freak-ness was a source of major contention with us. Steve didn't score a lot of points the first year we were married with his nagging about my efforts to clean our home.

Thankfully, somewhere along the line, my husband had a moment of enlightenment that he was the one with the unreasonable expectations. He had an epiphany that I wasn't trying to make him frustrated by not cleaning on top of the refrigerator or under the washer and dryer. Then, once he saw what the Scriptures said about selflessness, he started serving me by doing all the things himself that he was expecting me to do.

At that point, he started serving me in every way he could to make my life easier. And this was contagious because I saw how he wanted to serve me, and it made me want to serve him as well and look for things to make his life easier. The more we lay down our lives for each other, and the more we selflessly serve each other, the more sizzle we will have in our marriage!

Selflessness is a marriage principle that applies to both husband and wife. *"Submit to one another out of reverence for Christ"* (Ephesians 5:21). I've looked in a vast number of Bibles, and it's always the same. Verse 21 always comes before verse 22. So the principle of selfless submission is first applied to the husband and wife together.

Wives Submit to Your Husbands

Not until Ephesians 5:22-24 is submission explicitly applied to wives.

> *"Wives, submit yourselves to your own husbands as you do to the Lord. For the husband is the head of the wife as Christ is the head of the church, his body, of which he is the Savior. Now as the church submits to Christ, so also wives should submit to their husbands in everything."*

This scripture has been so misunderstood that many women bristle at the word submission. But God's plan is that the husband gives up his life (his desires) for his wife, putting her first, ministering to her and loving her as Christ loves the church. And likewise, the wife respects and ministers to her husband by putting him first because of her love for Christ. Then, as both husband and wife submit to one another there is a Christ-centered balance; they are both blessed, and the marriage sizzles.

I hope you notice that I've used the word "minister" to describe how we are to treat one another. I can't say it strongly enough...if we are married, our first and foremost ministry is to our spouse. When I think about ministering to Steve, I get excited about out-doing him in his service to me. I pray that God would give me creative ways to minister to him, to take care of him and to help make his life easier. And not just easier, but more fun and exciting. Sometimes we can get too serious doing all the things we think we need to do and we forget to have fun and enjoy ourselves. Steve's job can be stressful at times, so one way I try to minister to him is by making his life more fun.

The principle of submission is essentially walking in the way of Jesus in the context of marriage. We never demand submission from anyone. If anyone demands submission, the focus is on them, which is selfish, not selfless. The wife is to voluntarily offer submission in the same way that she voluntarily submits herself to the Lord. It is never to be imposed by the husband.

The Lord never hollers at us, "Submit to me!" Instead, he woos us, he loves us, he laid down his life for us, and he gave up everything for us. Then and only then, does he invite us to choose to submit to his loving lordship, which is exactly how God designed submission by the wife in marriage.

How can a wife submit to her husband?

• First, wives need to pray for their husbands. I remember years ago thinking about who was praying consistently for

Steve. I realized that this was a calling I dare not overlook. Steve needs my prayers! Prayer may be the most important thing wives ever do for their husbands. As a wife, I also need to pray that God helps me become the best wife I can be. If I try to act selflessly on my own strength, I can assure you that it will get old and I will burn out and feel resentful. I need the Holy Spirit to empower me to selflessly serve my husband.

- Another way a wife can submit to her husband is to look for ways to bless him. It brings me great joy to serve Steve. If you are not sure where to begin, then ask your husband what he would appreciate. This is all part of becoming a student of your husband. Study him closely to discover what makes him happy. This includes learning what pleases him in bed.

- One more way a wife can selflessly serve her husband is to speak well about him to others. I can't tell you how many times I've been with a group of women and it has turned into a complaint session about their husbands. Proverbs 31:12 says that a wife of noble character brings her husband good, not harm, all the days of her life. In part, this means speaking about our husbands with respect and love. A wife should never criticize her husband to others or in front of others. God wants us to build our husband up and to breathe greatness into him.

Husbands Love Your Wives

Steve—So, the wife certainly has a tough role to fill. But I think an even greater challenge is what the husband is called to do. In fact, this may be the most challenging verse in the entire Bible: *"Husbands, love your wives, just as Christ loved the church and gave himself up for her..."* (Ephesians 5:25). This is huge, and it's where the rubber meets the road. In my opinion, this is the most important key to a sizzling marriage. And it's all about selfless servanthood. Husbands are to love their wives as Christ loved the church and gave himself up for her.

In 40-plus years of marriage, every time I offer Pam a selfless love, every time I offer a love where I lay down my life just as Christ laid down his life, our relationship works brilliantly. But whenever I hang on to my rights, whenever I make it all about me, things go south quickly. Husbands, we have an enormous responsibility in marriage!

Years ago I read a quote by Richard Halverson who was Chaplain to the US Senate at that time. Halverson said that in all his years of ministry he had come to the conclusion that 90% of marriage problems stemmed from the husband's failure to love their wives as Christ loved the church. I am not sure if I agree with Halverson's exact percentage. But I do agree with him that husbands carry an extraordinary responsibility in marriage. I don't believe I have ever seen a marriage fail when the husband has genuinely laid down his life and loved his wife as Christ loved the church.

Marriage is not about controlling our spouse. It is about serving. A husband's role is to selflessly serve his wife. His role is to lay his life down for her, to give up his rights for her, to give up everything and even to die for her, if necessary, just like Christ did for us. This is servant-leadership in marriage. It is utterly selfless.

How can a husband show his wife selfless love?

• First, by diligently praying for his wife and asking God to empower him to be the husband she needs. A husband can also pray for wisdom and creativity. I have prayed relentlessly for these things throughout our marriage.

• A second way a husband can selflessly serve is by becoming a student of his wife. What does she like? What does she not like? What are her fears? What are her private thoughts? A husband can ask his wife questions about how she wants things done. I frequently ask Pam probing questions so that I can learn more about her. Loving our wives as Christ loved the church means listening to her, valuing her ideas and being tender toward her.

• Another way a husband can show selfless servanthood to his wife is to train his children to honor their mother. Children need to be taught to respect and honor their mother, and the primary person that teaches this important trait is their dad. Because of this, I never allowed our children to back-talk or be rude toward Pam.

• Loving our wife as Christ loved the church also means putting our wife before extended family, hobbies, and work. It means making the relationship with our wife our top priority. A frequent problem I have seen in my marriage counseling over the years is the wife feeling like she comes second. This is devastating in marriage. The greatest need for a wife is to feel loved, cherished and valued by her husband. She will only feel this if she is confident that she is the number one human relationship in her husband's life.

• Serving around the house is another way a husband can selflessly love his wife. A husband can help with the dishes, the laundry, the housework, bathing small children and getting them into bed. This has been a passion of mine for many years as I have served Pam over and over again.

• A husband must also learn to selflessly serve his wife in bed by putting her needs and wants above his own. Of course, this means helping her to reach orgasm before he does. But it also means husbands drawing their wives into a deeper intimacy with Jesus. If Christ is the groom and the church is the bride, then it suggests that the sexual relationship between a believing husband and wife is an illustration of God's enormous love for us. With this in mind, on occasion, I have prayed for Pam to experience God's love through me as we make love together. This is consummate selflessness.

Now, husbands should not do all this just to get something back from their wives. Instead, a Spirit-filled husband serves his wife because serving is how Christ loves us and it's how he wants us to follow in his footsteps. It isn't the easy way, but it's walking in the way of Jesus. Just · like Jesus loves us selflessly, husbands are also to love their wives selflessly.

Selflessness in marriage is the language of God's love. God loved us so much that he gave us his only Son, Jesus. The purest form of love is always a self-giving love. When Pam and I are at our best, this is what we experience. I give myself selflessly to her, and she gives herself selflessly to me. It is a phenomenal experience. And it is all part of a marriage that sizzles!

To wrap up this chapter on selflessly serving each other, we want to include two prayers: one for the husband and one for the wife. We encourage you to use these prayers as you continue in your journey toward a marriage that sizzles.

A Husband's Prayer

Heavenly Father, please forgive me for not walking consistently with you and for not loving you with all my heart. I am so prone to wander! Lord, I ask your forgiveness for not putting you first and foremost in every area of my life. Far too often I have run after my own wants, wishes, and desires instead of seeking you first above all else.

Lord, I confess that I have not always been the husband that you desire me to be. Many times I have not loved my wife as you love the church. For this, I am truly sorry. Please make me into the husband that you created me to be. I want to become the husband that my wife needs. I want to cherish her and shepherd her with a supernatural love that draws her to you. Help me to love my wife so richly that she sees through the lens of my love how deeply you love her.

Raise me up, O Lord, to be a reflection of Christ in my home and in my marriage. Help me to put aside my selfishness and to pour into my marriage so that it can become all that you desire! Help me to see how I can minister to my wife and help her to become all that you have created her to be.

Raise me up to be the shepherd of my home. Lord, please give me the kindness and tenderness of a shepherd toward my wife. Show me how to love her in ways that surprise her. Show me how to pray for her. Show me the things that distract me from loving my wife as you would have me love her. Give me the courage to make the changes necessary in our life together so that we can put you at the center of our marriage.

Start with my heart, O God! Start with me! Draw me, mold me and fill me with your Holy Spirit. Show me how to love my wife as Christ loves the church! Help me to give myself up for her. Please pour out your supernatural love on my wife through me. Help me to put her desires and needs before my own.

Lord, make our marriage strong and vital...a marriage that our family, friends, and neighbors would want to emulate. And when asked about our marriage, give me the boldness to share how Jesus makes all the difference.

Lord, I want to glorify you in my marriage. Yet I recognize that none of this is possible in my own strength. So I cry out to you, O God! I need your help! Please come with your mighty power and grant me these petitions.

In Jesus' name! Amen!

A Wife's Prayer

Heavenly Father, please forgive me for not walking consistently with you and for not loving you with all my heart. I am so prone to wander! Lord, I ask your forgiveness for not putting you first and foremost in every area of my life. Far too often I have run after my own wants, wishes, and desires instead of seeking you first above all else.

Lord, I confess that I have not always been the wife that you desire me to be. Many times I have not loved my husband as the church is to love Christ. For this, I am truly sorry. Please make me into the wife that you created me to be. I want to become the wife that my husband needs. I want to respect and love my husband with a supernatural love that draws him to you and shows him how much you also love him.

Raise me up, O Lord, to be a reflection of Christ in my home and in my marriage. Help me to put aside my selfishness and to pour into my marriage so that it can become all that you desire! Help me to make my husband my first ministry. Show me how to pray for my husband. Show me how to meet my husband's needs in every area of our relationship.

Please show me how to make our home a refuge, a place of peace and love so that my husband looks forward to coming home. Give me creative ideas how to encourage my husband. Please do not let me get distracted by the things of this world so that I forget my holy calling to minister to my husband.

Start with my heart, O God! Start with me! Draw me, mold me and fill me with your Holy Spirit. Make me content with what I have and help me to recognize what is truly important in life. Give me a thankful and receptive heart toward you.

Lord, make our marriage strong and vital...a marriage that our family, friends, and neighbors would want to emulate. And when asked about our marriage, give me the boldness to share how Jesus makes all the difference.

Lord, I want to glorify you in my marriage. Yet I recognize that none of this is possible in my own strength. So I cry out to you, O God! I need your help! Please come with your mighty power and grant me these petitions.

In Jesus' name! Amen!

Chapter Four

Secret #4

Forgive and Move Foreword

Pam—Every marriage goes through painful seasons. How can it be otherwise when we are all broken vessels in constant need of God's grace? For this reason, forgiving and moving forward is another indispensable key to experience a marriage that sizzles. Steve and I have lived this out firsthand many times. I have had to forgive Steve, and he has had to forgive me. The story we are about to share is undoubtedly the most painful time of forgiveness we have endured. And we share it to illustrate that with God's help, a marriage can overcome even the most tragic of circumstances.

When Steve and I decided to write this book about marriage we had to come face to face with sharing these events. We had not done so previously because of counsel given to us by Ben Merold, our pastor when these events took place. Ben met with us toward the end of a painful two-year journey. He told us something I have never forgotten.

He said, "The reason I have been willing to put you through all this pain is because I want you to be able to say, 'it was dealt with...it's over'...so you never have to bring it up again." Then Ben said to Steve, "Someone along the way may try to throw this in your face. It will probably be someone younger than you, but I want you to be able to say 'it's done...it's over...it's been dealt with.' Now, get yourself back to Chile and get back to the work God has called you to!"

As a result, Steve and I put this chapter completely behind us and have never brought it up publicly...until now. However, to experience a marriage that sizzles, to have a passion-filled marriage, requires both forgiving and moving forward. So we believe that God is now calling us to share the great miracle of grace and forgiveness that God has given us so that others can also be encouraged in their marriages. We want people to believe that even "the worst" in their marriage can also be overcome with God's grace.

Jesus was once asked how many times we are to forgive. His answer was breathtaking. *"I tell you, not seven times, but seventy-seven times"* (Matthew 18:22). In other words, stop counting! It's not about keeping score. Extending forgiveness is part and parcel to living in the way of Jesus. This is true for all of our relationships, but especially in marriage. *"Be kind and compassionate to one another, forgiving each other, just as in Christ God forgave you"* (Ephesians 4:32).

Forgiveness is not excusing inexcusable behavior. But it does release its hold on us. Forgiveness frees us from the anger and bondage that inevitably come from the bitterness that grows if we don't forgive. Philip Yancey, in his powerful book *What's So Amazing About Grace*, puts it like this. "Forgiveness alone can halt the cycle of blame and pain, breaking the chain of ungrace."

The truth is, when we've been offended, we are held prisoner to that offense until we release the one who perpetrated it against us. Often the one who forgives experiences even more freedom than the one who has been forgiven. I have experienced this freedom myself. For this reason, Steve and I firmly believe that forgiving and moving forward is an essential key to a marriage that sizzles.

Steve—With that said, one tragic night during August of 1985, I committed adultery. The consequences of this heinous sin blanketed the next two years of our lives and indelibly shaped our marriage. I will share what happened from my perspective and what lessons I learned. Pam will then share from her point of view. We are doing this because we both want you to know that God can redeem even the most tragic marriage situations, if we allow him to, by extending forgiveness and moving forward.

It was the winter of 1982 when we arrived in Chile to do the work we felt God was calling us to do, and we jumped in with both feet. I was 28 years old. Pam was 26. We were both zealous to make a difference for the cause of Christ. At other points in the book, we have shared about the passion we had to follow Jesus to the ends of the earth.

This fire-in-our-soul has been there throughout our marriage. It was, in fact, the primary reason Pam and I were attracted to each other. Jesus was first for us and the sky was the limit for how we imagined that God might use us.

Dwight L. Moody once said, "The world has yet to see what God will do with a man fully consecrated to him." With a great deal of naïveté (I now realize) but without any arrogance (as far as I knew), when we arrived in Chile, I dreamed that I could be just such a man and that Pam could be just such a woman. We were surrendered to Jesus and open to doing whatever he wanted us to do in Chile.

Not surprisingly, we dove into the work God had assigned us. The early years in Chile were joyously frenetic. We opened a literature distribution office and began resourcing more than 100 churches throughout our region. We started holding evangelistic campaigns. I hired a team of Chilean leaders who took our campaign tent and evangelistic resources throughout the nation.

The heyday of this ministry was 1985 when we held 50 one-week evangelistic campaigns throughout Chile. We held a campaign nearly every single week that year. More than 5,000 decisions for Christ were made. The impact was palpable. Even now, 30-plus years later, whenever I return to Chile someone will invariably approach to say they became a Christ follower "en la carpa"...in the tent.

In addition to those ministries, Pam and I both taught classes and preached in churches throughout our region. We also began building church buildings. I hired a construction foreman who kept a team of workers busy full time as we built one church after another. We loved our Chilean brethren, and we loved seeing God at work in such a revolutionary way. The cause of Christ in Chile's 5th Region was expanding in remarkable ways.

On top of that, we also began hosting college interns. These were groups of young people who were sent by our home church, Eastside Christian Church in Southern California, to spend two months with us in Chile. If the pace of life was delirious during regular seasons, it ramped up several notches when the interns were with us. The first year the interns came they had a self-contained translator... so I did not have to be with them 24-7. But in the following years, I was needed to translate which meant I was out almost every single night.

Looking back, it was absurd to the max. By this time, you must be thinking, "Steve and Pam, why didn't you see how foolish this was? What were you thinking?" But there are no excuses. Pam and I loved what we were doing, and we were both blind to our circumstances. You already know about the "train wreck," so you know what's coming. Eventually, my soul became parched, and I was vulnerable. In hindsight, I can see clearly with 20-20 vision. But at the time I was blinded...I couldn't see it—or maybe I didn't want to see it.

It was three years after arriving in Chile, and while Pam was in the USA, a woman showed up at the house one night unannounced and rang the doorbell. Pam's trip to the states was widely known and provided an opportune moment for Satan to strike. And I made the worst decision of my life by letting the woman in. When she left a short time later, I immediately realized the horrendously poor decision I had made. I repented with tears—something I would repeat many more times over the next two years.

The rest of that evening I asked God over and over to forgive me as I pleaded for his mercy...which I believe he gave me in that moment. My hope was that it would go no further, and I desperately prayed that God would spare my wife the pain of knowing that I had betrayed her. I hoped and prayed, too, that I would avoid the painful fires of discipline—but God had other plans.

I avoided the woman as much as possibe. A few weeks later, I was called back to the USA for an emergency meeting with our mission leadership. Shortly after, my father committed suicide, and I traveled back to the USA again. I had only been home a few days when our son Tommy was born, and our lives became consumed with caring for a new baby. Four months after Tommy's birth, we returned as a family to the USA on our first furlough. Up to this point, I assumed my private, heartfelt repentance was sufficient and that the consequences of my sin were behind me. But I was wrong.

In January 1987, after our furlough, my family and I returned to Chile. Days later, the husband of the woman came to our door, and it became immediately clear that I would face many more consequences for my sin. First and foremost was the thing I dreaded most; I had to tearfully confess to Pam what I had done and humbly beg for her forgiveness...which she graciously extended to me. Next, I called Eastside's mission's leadership on the phone and confessed my sin and repented. The tears were only beginning.

I still had to confess and repent to our Chilean church leaders. So, we held a tearful meeting at our house with about ten pastors and leaders. Once again I stood in shame as I confessed my sin and repented, and then asked for each person's forgiveness. After deliberating together, the Chilean leaders, one-by-one, looked me directly in the eyes and extended their gracious forgiveness. This was also when the leaders decided that I should not speak or teach publicly for six months as a disciplinary action for my sin.

These men also recommended that I receive extra pastoral care during this period of discipline, knowing full-well that I would need it. Not surprisingly, these beloved pastors began coming to our house every Tuesday morning to pray for me and to see how Pam and I were holding up. This act of love on their part developed into a special weekly prayer time that continued for many years, even after we moved thirty minutes away to live closer to our kids' schools.

Early on in this process, my precious wife went to the woman's house and personally told her that she had forgiven her. It was a brave and heroic step of faith for Pam, which gives you a glimpse into her amazing Christ-like character.

In June 1987, after six months of discipline, the Chilean leadership fully restored me to ministry and allowed me to resume speaking and teaching. At that point, Pam and I assumed the entire painful chapter was finally behind us. But there was more to come.

In July of that same year, and nearly two years after the sin took place, a delegation of Eastside's leadership came to Chile. With many more tears, they informed us that we had to return to the USA to address the open wounds my sin had created in our family and sending church. Needless to say, the Chilean pastors reacted quite negatively. They had not expected this reaction and felt my sin had been dealt with sufficiently and that I had completed my discipline with humility and submissiveness. They were fiercely supportive of us.

One heart-wrenching day was spent in a camp we occasionally used called El Tabo. Eastside's delegation was adamant. We had to return to the USA. The Chilean pastors pleaded with agonizing tears for that not to happen. I was caught in the middle translating between these two groups, both whom I loved with all my heart, with tears streaming down my face. I will never forget it, yet I realized fully that all of this pain had been because of me. God wanted to make sure I remembered the grievous consequences of sin!

At last, they finally reached a compromise, and everyone agreed. Pastor Melo (one of our key pastors) would be sent to the USA along with us, to inform Eastside's leadership in person that the Chilean pastors had already placed me under sufficient discipline. In their minds, my sin had been dealt with, and I had already been fully restored to go back into ministry. A few days later our entire family traveled back to the USA with Pastor Melo where even more pain was yet to come.

First, at a family gathering at my in-laws' house, I tearfully confessed my sin to Pam's parents and her three sisters and their husbands. I asked for each person's forgiveness...which they freely gave me, and there were many, many tears shed. Pastor Melo was also with us for the family meeting.

The next day, Pam and I appeared before a meeting of Eastside's elders and deacons (about 50 people were in the room). Again with tears and shame, I confessed my sin and asked their forgiveness. At this point, Eastside's mission leadership recommended that we be sent to Link Care, a specialized missionary counseling center in Fresno, CA, where we would be assessed as to whether or not we would be allowed to return to Chile. This course of action was agreed upon, and off we went to Link Care, along with Pastor Melo...who had continuously been an active voice of encouragement.

Our family spent about six weeks at Link Care. (Pastor Melo returned to Chile after the first week.) The Link Care team assessed us from every angle imaginable. We were tested, interviewed, received specialized counseling and took classes. Six weeks later, Brent Lindquist, co-founder of Link Care, flew down to Fullerton and presented a report to Eastside's elders and deacons. This was the same group that Pam and I had met with several weeks earlier.

Brent recommended that we be sent back to Chile fully restored. His only suggestion was that Eastside watch more carefully my tendency to over-work. Brent's recommendation carried the day and, shortly thereafter, we were headed back to Chile now serving as Field Director for Eastside's growing team of missionaries.

It was at that point that Eastside's Senior Pastor, Ben Merold, met with us. Pam has already shared what Ben said, but I have never forgotten his words. He said, "The reason I have been willing to put you through all this pain is because I want you to be able to say 'it was dealt with... it's over'....so you never have to bring it up again.'" Ben's words, along with a letter of reinstatement by Eastside's mission leadership, gave new life to my soul and our family traveled back to Chile with renewed energy.

So, what did I learn? Well, the most obvious lesson is that you can't hide sin. At some point God will always bring it to light. So confess sin early, repent and move forward.

An even more valuable lesson was that I needed to fiercely protect my marriage. Perhaps this is one reason that today Pam and I are almost fanatical about guarding our marriage and cultivating it so that it will be all that God intends.

Another lesson was that I had to forgive myself. This did not come quickly or easily. I had caused enormous pain and embarrassment to my wife, to my extended family, to my Chilean church leaders, to another Chilean family, and to my home church. It took many years before I began to believe "in my heart" that I was fully forgiven by God and by my family and friends.

The most critical step in this process was not giving up on God's calling on my life. At some points, it would have been easier to move back to the states and sell insurance (or something else unrelated to ministry). But doing that would have prevented God's work from becoming complete in my life. Forgiving myself and moving forward required that I take another step forward every day as a faithful husband and as a servant of God.

I also learned in a deeply profound way about grace. You may think that I was put through hell and that Eastside's leadership had no business doing what they did. But I would strongly disagree. I knew that all the people involved loved me and they only wanted my best—and our family's best.

Until he died, Sheldon Welch, Eastside's Mission Pastor, was a father figure to me. He loved me like a son, and it hurt him enormously to see Pam and me hurting. However, he knew what was necessary to put the situation completely behind us. I am who I am today, and Pam is who she is today, because Eastside believed in us and gave us a second opportunity.

Another lesson is one I have continued to learn over and over again...I married way above my league. Pam is a rock star!

Pam—When Steve mentioned that we could have never written a book on marriage without a chapter on this painful time, I wholeheartedly agreed. I'm sure these events have played a part in our cleaving to each other so tightly and in our awareness that there is no perfect family, nor perfect marriage. I won't repeat the details of the story. But I do want to give God the glory for what he did for us. God spared our marriage and also protected our children.

In Steve's story, he recounts our passion for the work and our hectic life in Chile. I was also a busy mother of three little girls and pregnant with our son Tommy. Looking back, perhaps we were trying to prove that we were "great missionaries." But the reality is both of us felt that we were doing exactly what we were supposed to be doing.

Steve wrote lengthy, weekly letters to Eastside, our sending church, but there was no one on-the-ground in Chile to hold us accountable. There was no one close enough to see how bone-weary tired we were both becoming. I recall Steve returning from an intense two-week evangelism trip into northern Chile with our college interns in July 1985. This was only a few weeks before the sin. Steve had lost about 20 pounds (which in those days he could ill-afford to lose), and he looked like death-warmed-over.

I was shocked when he came through the door. Exhaustion doesn't even begin to describe what he looked like. It should have been a massive warning for both of us, but there was no one around to give us council or to provide perspective. We were both blind to what was happening to us and how tired we had become.

Still, we did not come to grips with all of this until a year and a half later. In January of 1987, we had just returned to Chile from furlough. We had been back in our Chilean home for only a few days when Steve confessed to me what had happened 18 months earlier. The outpouring of grace, love, and support from the Chilean pastors with whom we worked was incredible.

But I had to work through anger, betrayal, embarrassment, and fear. This was a high priority for us in the ensuing months. My husband and I spent an abundant amount of time together. We took long walks and shared deeply. Where were we going? What were the most important things in our lives? How were we going to be intentional about healing our marriage and developing healthy boundaries as a couple?

I also had to be strong for our four children. I was a busy

mother of four little ones. During that time we made family time in the evenings a high priority. Steve began to schedule any evening meetings after the children were in bed. We also took more intentional breaks to re-evaluate our schedules throughout the year.

In addition, I had to be strong for the ministry God had entrusted to us. I loved the work God had called us to in Chile. When Steve's sin was exposed, I had a considerable amount of fear that our ministry would end. It never even occurred to me that our marriage might also end. Perhaps this was because Steve was so repentant and that the circumstances, though wrong, gave me hope that we could survive. I'm confident the grace and love from our Chilean pastors also helped to provide me with the hope and strength I needed.

So I did the right thing and forgave Steve and then moved forward one step at a time. I'm sure had we been living in the USA, I would have gone to a counselor to work through some of the underlying feelings that were locked up under the guise of "doing the right thing." But at the time, with the self-awareness I had, I resolved my feelings in the best way I knew how. And God met me in profound ways. I cried out to him, and he carried me through those months. His presence, his Word, his faithfulness and his healing hand were all very evident.

Our home church, Eastside, spent an enormous amount of time, effort and money to fully restore us. They believed in us, and their love for us was shown by their huge investment in our healing. As I look back, I realize how beautiful it was to see Christians give grace so freely and to work so diligently for restoration.

The time at Link Care was a positive experience, that is, until one day I was sitting in a "class" with some other missionary wives, and I realized that I was in a group therapy session. I was horrified that I was there. I was still young and thought I had dealt with my issues and didn't need to be there. Looking back, I realize I had a lot of pride that clouded my realization of the desperate situation I was in.

Steve and I had to talk a lot, pray a lot and work through things. We had to forgive and move forward. Over the years I have had to deal periodically with recurring hurt from that time. It was like one layer of the onion skin would be removed and then, over time, something else would come up that would take me back to those painful days, and then another layer of onion skin would be peeled off.

More prayer, more talking, more forgiving and more moving forward. It was a process for me. I have always been better at taking care of everyone else and pushing my own feelings and needs aside. So, I busied myself with our children and the part of the work that I did with the women in Chile. I had not learned how to stop and allow myself time to grieve and to take care of me. This is something I have had to learn over the years—and I'm still learning.

I do remember God showing up in a powerful way in those first months back in Chile. After being in the USA for eight months, getting back into speaking Spanish was a challenge for me. But during that time when I asked God to give me a supernatural ability to express my feelings in Spanish, he was faithful to give it to me. I was even surprised how I was able to say things in Spanish that I normally would not have been able to say—and the fluidity was amazing. I knew it was God.

I also remember reading through the Minor Prophets. And God spoke to me so clearly! He ministered to me in profound ways through that portion of his Word. I laughed at the thought that I could get so much out of the Minor Prophets! It goes to show that God can use anything! I didn't have women to go to in Chile for help or counsel—but God held me together. Once we came back to the USA and Steve confessed to my family, everyone rallied around us in ways I never imagined, and they were very supportive.

Burn-out is real. When enough time goes by without refueling, and you are living on fumes, then your perspective, your defenses, and your motivations are clouded. I'm not giving excuses; I am merely sharing how I have dealt with a one-time event. It wasn't an on-going affair. There was true repentance. Steve repented from his sin, walked through the discipline with humility and was restored fully to ministry.

This entire episode has given us both more grace for others who have fallen into temptation and made us set up boundaries in ministry and in our marriage that have been guardrails throughout the ensuing years. This part of our journey is something I would never have chosen. But it is real life stuff that many married couples go through. Not everyone endures the depth of betrayal that I did, but every marriage faces disappointments and wounds. Whenever that happens, we have a choice to make. In my case, I chose to forgive and move forward. I chose my husband.

That being said, when we've been deeply hurt, forgiveness

is often not a glib "once and done" step. It also becomes an ongoing choice. As memories resurface, we may have to choose over and over to declare that we have already forgiven the offense and that Jesus' blood was indeed sufficient.

It is also important to note that some offenses may require several layers of forgiveness. For example, the act of infidelity is only one issue. But there may also be a need to seek forgiveness for dishonoring your spouse, for breaking the marriage vow, and for any other ramifications caused by the sin. It is helpful to verbalize these layers of forgiveness to the offended party so that complete healing and restoration can begin.

I remember someone once telling me they thought that infidelity was something you could never get over. But after hearing what we went through, they realized that it is possible for a marriage to have restoration from any circumstance... provided both the husband and wife are willing to forgive and move forward.

What Satan meant for harm, God turned into something good, and I am incredibly thankful that we stuck it out and worked hard to make things right between us. Romans 8:28

is true. *"And we know that in all things God works for the good of those who love him, who are called according to his purpose."* Our entire marriage has been a testament of God's grace. For this, I am eternally thankful!

I don't know what you may have been through in your marriage. But I do know this: God's grace and mercy are always greater. And I also know from personal experience that a vital key to a sizzling marriage is to forgive and move forward.

Chapter Five

Secret #5

Enjoy Lingering Conversations

Pam—Steve and I have discovered another secret to a truly sizzling marriage is what we now refer to as lingering conversations. Over thirty years have passed since the dark chapter in Chile. Throughout those years we have discovered many things that have contributed to healing, growth and deepening passion in our relationship—but lingering conversations may be the most important.

Lingering conversations provide time and space to open up about what is going on inside us. These conversations occur when we have extended time together after we are done talking about the day-to-day details of life. Lingering conversations happen when we are comfortable with long moments of silence sitting together in the same room. They happen when we feel free enough with each other to think out loud, to share dreams and to express ideas that are not fully developed.

When I listen to struggling wives and hear how little time they spend on their marriage relationship, I often wonder if the couple really even knows each other. Life can be so busy that we don't invest time sharing what is going on inside us. I don't mean sharing about how our day went...but opening up so that our spouse knows what we are dealing with, thinking about, pondering, fearing and dreaming. This type of deeper conversation does not happen when kids are vying for our attention at the dinner table, or when we are in a hurry to get somewhere, or frustrated about something, or when we have an agenda.

For Steve and I, lingering conversations have become almost as important to us as sex—in fact, one often leads to the other! (But I don't want to get ahead of myself.) First, let me share one of the prerequisites to engage in a lingering conversation.

Freedom From Resentment

It may sound simple, but to have a beautiful, soul-baring lingering conversation a married couple needs to be as free as possible from resentment toward one another. Unhealed hurts and raw wounds will prevent us from opening up to each other. If I am miffed at Steve, the last thing I want to do is be vulnerable with him. The same is true for him. If Steve has pent-up resentment toward me, there is no way we'll find the "sweet spot" that leads to a lingering conversation.

Learning to release resentment did not come easily for me. I had to learn to speak my mind and share my feelings with Steve. Several years ago I reached a point where I was not happy with our status quo. So I told Steve that we needed "a new dance step"...a new way of communicating. The things that had "worked" in our marriage for the previous decades were not working any longer.

All relationships have a "dance." This is the way we communicate, the way we interact with each other, the way we move in our relationship. In our case, after decades dancing in a certain rhythm, I realized that I needed to be heard more and to express my needs more clearly. It's possible that before this breakthrough I may not have even been aware of some of my needs. However, once the ice was broken, I discovered an entirely new voice to express what I was learning about myself.

I believe all marriages have ebbs and flows, ups and downs, and as we work through the tough times, the "dance" changes. When I was finally able to tell Steve what I didn't like and what I really wanted and how certain things in our relationship made me feel, then he was able to understand me exponentially better.

For years we had asked each other, "How can I be a better wife or husband?" This thoughtful mindset was healthy, yet for us, it was incomplete. The missing link was my inability to express myself. Instead of building up resentment toward my husband's behavior, what I needed was to let him know what bothered me and what changes I wanted in our "dance." Fortunately, Steve listened and was willing to make these changes, but it was quite a story how it all happened. Let me explain...

A number of years ago, I had allowed resentment to build. It came to a head while we were celebrating our anniversary. Over a fancy anniversary dinner, we got into a huge argument. I don't even remember what the fight was about, but we were both so furious that the second half of our meal was spent in total silence—so was the walk back to our hotel room, and so was our hotel room that night, as well as the long drive home the next morning.

When we got home, instead of unpacking my suitcase, I started putting some other things in it. I remember being so mad that I could hardly speak. Our anniversary celebration had been ruined! Steve sat in the chair watching me, totally bewildered as I told him I needed a break and that I was going somewhere.

And I did. I checked into a hotel in town. As all this was unfolding, I was having an out-of-body experience and thinking, "Pam, what are you doing?" I certainly was not leaving Steve, nor was I ending the marriage. I was just frustrated that we couldn't communicate in a way that would solve some of the issues we were dealing with. Yes, I was menopausal. However, I was also fed up, and I wanted some things to change.

I found myself in the hotel room wondering what in the world I had been thinking. Sitting there alone on the bed, I had plenty of time to pray and time to think about what changes I wanted in our marriage. Then I called Steve and told him that if he wanted to visit me, he could. Sheesh! What drama...and believe it or not, I am NOT a drama queen!

A short time later, there was a knock on the door. When I opened it, Steve was standing there, smiling. I was surprised that he had dressed up. Hmmm. This was something different, and I liked it. After a while, I finally opened up and shared my feelings. I explained to him how I had not felt listened to; how I had not felt that I was a high enough priority to him, and how I had not felt genuinely loved by him. On top of that, I was hurt that our anniversary celebration had been ruined.

Steve apologized and so did I. As we talked that evening, I realized it was the beginning of a new "dance" in our communication. Steve realized that I need him to look me in the eyes and give me more fully his attention. He also realized in a fresh way that I need to feel valued by him and that I need to know that he appreciates my thoughts and ideas. On the other hand, I also realized that part of the responsibility for our struggle was mine. Steve is not a mind-reader. For him to know my feelings, I need to share in a way that he can understand.

We talked for several more hours in the hotel room, but it was getting late, and we were both exhausted. That was when I asked my husband if he wanted to spend the night with me. To my delight, he said "Yes!" Thankfully, our room wasn't as quiet that night as it had been the previous evening!

There have been entire books written about how to deal with resentment. However, at the end of the day, the most critical step for Steve and I has simply been offering forgiveness. We have both done countless things to offend and hurt one another...some we have already discussed.

And although you may not pass through the same fires of pain that we have, every marriage will experience wounds. How can it be otherwise since we are such fallen people! Someone once put it like this: "Broken people always end up hurting broken people." Nowhere does this hold more true than in marriage.

Because of this, Steve and I have had to forgive each other over and over to be free from resentment. And, every so often, we have also changed our "dance steps" to reach new levels of communication. These choices have helped to open the doors for us to experience what we now affectionately call lingering conversations.

No Hidden Agenda and Trust

Steve—Another prerequisite for lingering soul-to-soul conversations is for neither spouse to have a hidden agenda. This means there is a settled peace between the husband and wife. Nothing is hidden. It helps a great deal when you not only love your mate but you also really like them. This is undoubtedly the case with us. Pam and I are absolutely wild about each other. What we experience together in our marriage is nothing short of phenomenal!

For us to reach this place in our relationship has required

working through many difficulties. We still get annoyed with each other at times—it would be abnormal if we didn't. It is usually a trivial issue that provokes a problem: a missed phone call, an overlooked chore, something expected not done. But since we are human, and at times we are tired or hungry or just plain selfish, the one who usually gets the curt word or the sharp tone or the disgusted look is our spouse.

Thankfully, Pam and I have both learned to apologize more quickly these days. This opens the door to clear out any hidden agendas and paves the way for our lingering conversations. The more we experience the pleasure of these soul-to-soul conversations the more we have determined to resolve quickly any differences that may arise—we don't want to waste any more days in pettiness and miss the sweet spots.

Trust is another prerequisite for a lingering conversation. Trust is vital because to open up to each other, Pam and I must feel safe that we can bare our soul with no fear of being laughed at or judged or called foolish. We also have to be confident that our spouse is truly interested in hearing what is going on inside us. This goes both ways. I need Pam to show interest and empathy when I open my heart to her, and she also needs me to show interest and empathy when she opens her heart to me.

Trust must be nurtured. And, with time, Pam and I have also discovered that it can be completely re-built even when it has been violated.

Remember when you and your spouse dated and you talked for hours on end? How in the world did you ever talk for two hours on the phone? How did you have that much to say? It's because you wanted to know each other better and be connected—even over the phone. But after a few years of marriage with too-busy schedules, children, work, the distractions of paying bills and other real-life issues, those cherished extended conversations become distant history because the urgent has taken precedent.

Often what results is a couple who may get along "on the outside," but they may not have a clue what's going on "inside" each other. This is why a couple of times a year, Pam and I take time away to be alone. These getaways are times of rest, to be quiet and to nurture the trust in our relationship. When we get away, we usually have no agenda other than to be together. We may read a book together or separately. We may take naps together or separately. We may go for walks, sit in a hot tub, or lounge by the pool.

We ask questions of each other, and we listen to the answers and gain insights. When we are away like this, we know that we can be ourselves. We don't have to prove anything or look a certain way. We can think out loud and know that the other will be patient for us to verbalize and understand how we feel. Trust grows because there are no sarcastic comments, rolling of the eyes and critical responses. It also grows because there is acceptance, unconditional love, and undivided attention.

Manageable Stress Levels

Pam—Stress is inevitable in life, but too much stress will severely limit the possibility of having lingering conversations and any potential ensuing romance. We have learned this many times over the years.

An early example happened when we were new missionaries. Our daughter Christina had been ill for most of our six months while attending language school in Costa Rica. Because of this, I was especially fearful of coming to Chile at the beginning of winter with its cold and rainy weather.

As we arrived in Chile, Steve and I were both deeply concerned that Christina didn't repeat the chronic bronchitis cycle we had finally overcome as we were preparing to leave Costa Rica. But God, in his sovereignty, had a marvelous house waiting for us to rent in Chile and within days we moved in. A few days later our crate arrived from the USA, and we were able to get settled.

Honestly, I didn't feel like I was under stress. In fact, it was quite exciting—all the newness of our new home country. We were finally in the place we had been preparing for. But I kept losing weight, so much so, that I looked like a skeleton with clothes on. And I couldn't keep anything in my stomach.

This went on for several weeks until another missionary wife took me to the doctor and I was given some medicine for a digestive disorder that had been prompted by stress. The doctor's remedy: after two days of eating nothing, he told me I could only eat ice cream for the next two days. (Nice diet, don't you think? I chose chocolate.) Slowly I began eating food again, but only after taking a prescription pill before my meals.

This was a valuable lesson for us as we learned the devastating effects of stress. It can rob our health and erode marriage vitality—especially lingering conversations.

Because I didn't feel well during that season, Steve and I were not able to enjoy much romance or warmth in our relationship. And that is definitely not God's plan for marriage!

As the years have passed, Steve and I have learned to be much more attentive to the effects of stress. This has been particularly important because ministry is filled with stress-producing challenges. In the face of these challenges, we have made it our goal to keep our stress levels manageable so that we have adequate emotional margin for lingering conversations and romance.

Along the way, we have discovered four excellent stress relievers. These are not new, but they work. I'm referring to rigorous exercise, a healthy diet, adequate rest and ongoing spiritual communion with Jesus. Steve and I both have experienced the benefits of consistent, rigorous exercise. Now, I have to admit that Steve is a bit more disciplined in this area than me. But we both exercise strenuously several times a week. Steve is an avid swimmer, and I go to the gym. Exercise has repeatedly been proven to be an essential stress reliever.

Diet is also critical to relieving stress. I buy as much organic food as possible. We eat simple, healthy meals with reasonable proportions. We steer clear of too much salt and sugar. These are simple steps that help reduce stress.

We have already mentioned rest, but it bears repeating. Steve and I are in bed for eight to nine hours a night. We make no apologies for the rest we need to function at peak levels. God did not design us to live constantly tired and worn out. Many studies have shown that people today are too-frequently sleep deprived. One of the best things you can do for your marriage is to get enough rest!

Finally, investing consistent time in prayer, personal Bible study and communion with God is another stress reliever. As we mentioned in the opening pages of this book, marriage flourishes best when Christ is at the center. This requires both husband and wife to cultivate robust, ongoing Christ-centered lives. This begins with consistent prayer, personal Bible study and abiding communion with Jesus.

A Christ-centered life has many benefits, including reducing stress. Once again, this is vital because managing stress is a prerequisite for lingering conversations.

Time Alone Together

Steve—This leads to another prerequisite for lingering conversations—time alone together. When Pam and I were dating, like most couples, we went through all kinds of gyrations to be alone together. But this can flip after several years of marriage, and some couples eventually seem like they never want to be alone. We know married couples who invite friends to join them on every weekend away, and every vacation is spent with others. That's okay some of the time. But Pam and I are amazed at how many married couples never seem to spend any time alone.

Awhile back, Pam and I were meeting with a couple after we had just spent an entire week away. At the time, these people had been married about 20 years, and they wanted to know about our vacation. We told them that we rested, we read, we relaxed, we drank wine, we talked, we took long walks, we explored the area and we spent the entire time alone together. (We also had lots of wonderful sex, but we didn't tell them.) We assumed they would "get it." But they didn't. They looked at us dumbfounded and said, "Well, we could never do that! We would be bored to death!"

Now, I realize that different people enjoy different things, and I would not want to impose my style of relaxation on someone else. However, the bottom line is this—Pam and I have benefitted greatly by spending a generous amount of time alone together…the more romantic the location, the better! As a result, we enthusiastically encourage married couples to spend time alone to talk, to dream, to share thoughts and feelings, to discover new things about each other and to encourage each other. These things often happen in lingering conversations.

Lingering conversations are encouraged when we don't have to watch the clock. When my wife and I go out to dinner for a "real date," we look for a place where we can have what we call a "lingering meal." This place is somewhere with a private table, where others can't hear what we are saying. We start out sharing an appetizer and a glass of wine. Then we share a salad, split the main dish and split the dessert. This turns the dinner into a two-hour event. We enjoy deciding together what we are going to eat. We savor each course, take our time and make the evening last. This also allows time to discuss things that don't normally get talked about.

The rich conversations that happen over a lingering meal can also occur while taking a long walk or hike, or traveling for hours in a car, or laying in a hammock together. These conversations probably won't happen in a noisy sports bar with television screens creating distractions in every direction. It may seem obvious, but location matters. Private, quiet locations are best. If the setting is also romantic, that's even better! Location matters because lingering conversations require our full and undivided attention.

You might say, "I don't know what to talk about." Probing questions are always helpful. Ask about feelings and events during childhood. Try to get beyond the superficial. The Internet offers many helpful lists of questions for married couples. Once a question is asked, then listen carefully to the response. Probe with follow-up questions. This is sometimes referred to as "active listening." A good listener is never passive. Instead, a good listener actively engages with eye contact and insightful questions to learn as much as possible from the speaker.

Think back to your childhood best friend. More than likely, you were on the same communication wavelength. Good friends know how to read each other, and they communicate well. This is why lingering conversations involve much more than merely the words we choose. It's also the way we say them. Proverbs 15:1 says, "*A gentle answer turns away wrath, but a harsh word stirs up anger.*" The same words can be shared with a loving look and a tender voice or with an irritated look and a sarcastic tone. This is why it's so important to learn to speak and to listen with wisdom.

Timing is also important. For example, when I am speaking on a weekend, Pam will wait until Sunday afternoon to tell me some things. She knows I don't need another burden before speaking. Sometimes, when we're both exhausted, it's just not the time to try to hash out feelings of frustration or disappointment. So we wait until we're more rested—but we don't wait too long—maybe a day or two. This is where the Holy Spirit helps us to know how long to wait and how to best approach sensitive topics.

It is also very important to communicate feelings. Lingering conversations have been a helpful platform for us to open up about things that move us emotionally. Pam and I learned years ago to express ourselves like this: "When you do this or when you say that, it makes me feel…" When we speak like that, we are not attacking, but we are helping the other person to know how we feel about what they did or what they said. Addressing issues like this helps the other person not to get defensive because the main thing we are doing is clarifying how we feel.

Ultimately, lingering conversations are about the

journey, not a specific destination. The goal is to discover more intimately the amazing person God has called you to share life with. Once again these cannot be rushed, and they cannot be manufactured. Lingering conversations will only surface if you provide the time and space for them. A glass of wine also helps!

Pam—A while back, Steve let me know that we were going to host a dinner meeting in our home on a Sunday evening. That same weekend we were going to be in Boise, ID visiting his mother. Since we would be driving eight hours back from Boise to Reno on Sunday, I shared my concern that it might be a bit much for us to host a dinner for 16 at our house that same evening. Then he said matter-of-factly that we would get up very early on Sunday morning, and be back in Reno in plenty of time to receive our guests.

I defensively shot back that I was the one responsible for the main course for the dinner. My husband retorted that he remembered a family friend years ago who prepared a meal a month before a dinner meeting she had planned (and then stored it in the freezer) because she was going to be out of the country until right before the engagement. At that point, I ended the conversation because it was quickly going south.

Later on, when I brought it back up, I was able to share with Steve how his expectations for us to drive eight hours from Boise and then host a dinner meeting for 16 people made me feel overwhelmed. Once I was able to communicate my feelings, it helped Steve to understand how all of his carefully laid plans were impacting me.

He ended up changing our plans, and we flew to Boise, arriving back home with several hours to prepare for the dinner and the main course—which ended up being a very workable solution. However, it wasn't until Steve understood my feelings that he was able to see how unrealistic his initial plans were.

There is no escaping the fact that good communication takes time and effort, especially if we hope to experience lingering conversations. We need to invest enough time to unpack our feelings in ways that are helpful. If we are running at full speed for any length of time, this won't happen.

Communication also involves listening well. James 1:19 says, *"My dear brothers and sisters, take note of this: everyone should be quick to listen, slow to speak and slow to become angry…"* Sometimes we think that listening is a passive activity where we can just sit back and let everyone else take the responsibility to communicate clearly with us. But nothing is further from the truth. Listening well requires effort and focus to make sure we can actually hear the message that's intended.

One of the most helpful verses regarding communication is Ephesians 4:29. *"Do not let any unwholesome talk come out of your mouths, but only what is helpful for building others up according to their needs, that it may benefit those who listen."* If we consistently applied this verse, it would help our communication at every level, especially with lingering conversations in marriage.

Give the Benefit of the Doubt

Steve—Another key to lingering conversations is to give the benefit of the doubt. This principle comes out of a text that is read in many weddings—1 Corinthians 13. *"Love is patient, love is kind. It does not envy, it does not boast, it is not proud. It is not rude; it is not self-seeking..."* The text continues until it says, *"love bears all things, believes all things, hopes all things, endures all things."* To *"believe all things"* simply means that we give the benefit of the doubt until proven otherwise.

This is incredibly important for any healthy relationship, but especially if a husband and wife want to experience sizzle in their marriage. The reason this is important is that we are all broken people, and we will inevitably disappoint each other. Every so often there will be gaps between what we expected would happen and what actually does happen. And if we can fill those gaps by giving each other the benefit of the doubt, it's a game changer.

Pam and I shared earlier that we didn't know how to communicate well when we first got married. It was something we had to learn. And a lot of that was by trial and error. Every step of the way we've needed to give each other the benefit of the doubt. So, when Pam says something irritating, I try to stop before I react and ask myself, "What is really going on here? She is not usually like this; something must be bothering her." That's giving her the benefit of the doubt.

Likewise, if I snap back at her for some reason, Pam has a choice. Either she can react negatively and escalate the situation, or she can recognize that snapping back is not my "normal response" so there must be something else going on inside me. When we give each other the benefit of the doubt it allows us to catch ourselves before we get defensive, irritated, or mad—so we can find out what is really going on.

Pam—One time Steve miscalculated our finances. This miscalculation represented a few hundred dollars, which meant he had to dip into savings to make up the difference. When I first heard about it, I could have reacted and gotten all spooled up. But the fact is, I know that he is very careful with our money and rarely makes a mistake in this area. So, instead of getting angry, I thought to myself, "This is not the way he normally operates. There must be something else going on. Maybe he was just moving too quickly." In that moment, I was giving him the benefit of the doubt. I did not jump to conclusions that would have made things worse.

The truth is all of our relationships would improve if we stop jumping to conclusions and stop making premature assumptions, but this is especially helpful in marriage. To do this, we need to learn to ask questions and clarify, clarify, clarify. But the only way this can happen is to first give the benefit of the doubt.

With that said, I have to be honest by saying that our lingering conversations have become much deeper as we have weathered the struggles of life. Through the years, as we have experienced disappointments with each other and with those outside our marriage, we have grown in our faith, and our marriage has deepened. In many of those hard times, it would have been easy to grow apart, build walls and begin going through the motions in our marriage relationship. But I am thankful that Steve and I kept working on "us."

Having dry times in marriage is normal. It is normal not to see eye to eye on some things and to have disagreements. One thing I wish we did differently is to disagree as a couple more in front of our children. We tried to "protect" them by going into another room to disagree where they wouldn't hear us.

I realize now that it would have been more helpful if they had seen us occasionally argue. I think it would have been better for our kids to have seen us work through our differences to see that a healthy marriage works through disagreements, learns to compromise, argues respectfully and repeats often the phrases: "I'm sorry, and I forgive you." I regret that we did most of that hard work as a married couple behind closed doors where our kids could not witness how we handled our differences and how we resolved them.

After more than 40 years of marriage, I am still learning new things about Steve. And he is still learning things about me. That is because we take time to have lingering conversations. These are an avenue that God has given us to know each other better. Lingering conversations are a way to think out loud and have our spouse listen in, not to fix anything, but to encourage by listening. Lingering conversations sometimes enable us to answer our own questions. They help us to hear God more clearly, and they allow us to touch the soul of our spouse in a very profound way. Our prayer for you is that you and your spouse will have many cherished lingering conversations.

Chapter Six

Secret #6

Intentionally Invest in Your Marriage

Pam—We don't know where we learned this, but Steve and I have always believed that our marriage relationship comes first after our relationship with God. As a result, we have long advocated that every married couple needs to intentionally invest in their marriage. We have learned that this is another vital secret to a marriage that sizzles.

Our commitment to intentionally invest in our marriage has been illustrated in our daily rhythms for many years. Most days when Steve comes home from work, he and I sit on the couch for about fifteen minutes to discuss our day. Even when we had young children around, Steve and I took time to be together. We nourished our relationship, and we wanted to model that for our children. We went on date nights and once a year we went on a trip with just the two of us. We told our kids that we would return from the trip as "a better mommy and daddy." And we were!

I remember returning from those trips feeling like my emotional tank was full and I was a better wife and mother. Life looked healthier to me because I was emotionally healthier. Steve and I always found someone to watch our children, and the kids rose to the occasion because they felt secure in our family. The key point is that we intentionally invested in our relationship by getting away and finding the money to make those trips memorable.

One trip stands out because it was so exotic. Our second year in Chile as missionaries (before we went into ministry overdrive), we were able to purchase an incredible deal for five days in Rio de Janeiro, Brazil. Rio was beyond fun! The trip package included a host of tours and experiences.

One evening our entire tour group went to the Ballet Folklorico...which we were told would be a sample of typical Brazilian cultural dances. However, once we got there (and we were with a tour group so we couldn't leave), we discovered the program was a grand display of colorful costumes, lively music, and half-naked women. Steve and I turned three shades of red!

On another tour in Rio, we were taken by sailboat to an island where we were served a delicious lunch. I believe this was a tour to advertise a hotel that we could visit on our next trip to Brazil—which, by the way, we're still waiting for!

After lunch, I recall having a giant parrot roost on my arm. It was quite a sight. I often reminisce about our trip and being in the sailboat with its full sails cutting through the dark blue ocean waters. It was breathtaking.

Brazil was a trip of a lifetime, full of adventure and fun! It was also a wonderfully renewing time for our marriage with memorable and passionate intimacy. We had been busy for months with three little girls (ages 3½ and under), as well as a full plate of ministry responsibilities. But we returned home to Chile as better friends, more deeply in love, and much better parents.

Another trip that stands out was in Wisconsin. Steve and I spent a few days alone in beautiful Door County. We stayed in a lovely bed and breakfast with a fireplace in the room. I told Steve that I thought a fireplace in the master bedroom was the most romantic thing in the world. A few years later when we lived in Nevada, Steve remembered me saying this, and he had a fireplace put in our master bedroom. He scored many points for that!

Unfortunately, I hear more and more about how some parents let their children become the center of their universe, and refuse to leave them to go on a date. It's unsettling when parents can't even have a meaningful conversation because they allow the children to interrupt and run the show. I am stunned at the number of young moms who tell me that they could never leave their child overnight with anyone. Quite frankly, I believe that the children are running many of those homes. And the kids are quite happy with this arrangement because, after all, our carnal nature always wants to be in control.

Not surprisingly, what often suffers is the marriage relationship. Not to mention that those demanding children never learn one of the most important lessons of life...that we are NOT the center of the universe. I can't tell you how many young moms I have challenged to get their young children out of the marriage bed and make them sleep in their own bed. I've also urged them to find a good babysitter or trade babysitting with a friend, so they can go out with their husband to show him that he is important. What I have seen more times than I care to admit is that children take all the energy, focus, time and emotional wherewithal, and there is nothing left for the marriage relationship.

What is frequently overlooked is how beneficial it is for children when they sense the security of their parent's marital love. Children flourish in the fertile soil of a healthy marriage relationship. Kids thrive when they sense that mom and dad are united. When mom and dad are pulling in the same direction, children tend to be happier and feel safer.

This is why I believe that intentionally investing in our marriage is not selfish. Quite the opposite in fact; it can be one of the best gifts we give our children! Of course, I suppose this could also be taken to an unhealthy level, where mom and dad become so self-absorbed that they completely ignore their children. But, fortunately, that's not the norm. Still, in many cases, husbands and wives simply do not intentionally invest sufficient time and energy in their marriage. This is tragic because intentionality in the marriage relationship benefits immeasurably both the couple and their children.

Be Intentional About Get-Away Trips

Steve—As the years have passed, Pam and I are now even more intentional about investing in our marriage, which has resulted in even more sizzle in our relationship. At this stage in our lives, a few times a year we leave town to be alone as a couple. Since we live very active and public lives as a result of our ministry, when we "go away" we look for quiet, secluded places where we enjoy anonymity. When possible, we also like to find locations where we are inaccessible by the Internet. This allows Pam and I to have uninterrupted time to talk for hours on end, to read, pray, and be intimate.

We recently spent a week together after Easter resting on the Northern California coast. (Easter weekend is a huge push at our church with many extra services.) Several years ago we discovered an idyllic coastal community called Sea Ranch, about an hour north of Bodega Bay. We enjoy it so much, in fact, that we have returned to Sea Ranch several times, staying in rental homes so we can be alone. Pam and I wake up whenever we want, eat whenever we want, and slow down to reconnect with God and with each other.

We have found it helpful to carve out time regularly for us to do this. We've stayed in rental properties in a variety of locations—the more secluded, the better! Once we stayed in a tiny bungalow located in the middle of thirty acres of pristine forest, adjacent to a gloriously flowing river. The one-room cabin had massive windows on all four sides— with no curtains. It felt like we were in a human terrarium with the forest and river close enough to touch. At night, it seemed almost like we were sleeping under the stars in the open air, instead of being in a comfortable bed warmed by a wood burning stove.

A moment ago Pam shared how our marriage comes first after our relationship with God. One way we live this out is by "dropping out" from our workday world and responsibilities to reconnect soul-to-soul (and body to body!) with no distractions. It's incredible the depth of conversation that flows between us when there are no meetings to attend or emails to answer. Often we read books aloud to each other. Over the years we have read fiction, history, psychology and Christian books. Reading aloud gives us ample fodder for meaty conversations leading us to connect in fresh ways.

We also spend time alone reconnecting with God. While we are on these "escapes," both of us have extended times in prayer and reading our Bibles. We have time to think without any distractions. We go on hikes. We experience God's creation with rested eyes and refreshed souls. And, of course, this opens the door for us to experience the "act of marriage" in rejuvenating and celebratory fashion.

I have often said that no one can "have it all." Whenever we say "yes" to something, it means we are saying "no" to something else. Pam and I have chosen to make our marriage our first priority, after our relationship with God. And we both enjoy the sizzling results! We believe this is what God wants for other couples, too. At times I've said tongue-in-cheek that Pam and I have so much fun together it should be illegal. But it all stems from our decision to be intentional in our marriage—making it our first priority, after God.

Be Intentional About Your Words

Pam—Another way that we are intentional in our marriage is to stick up for each other. Not only am I Steve's greatest cheerleader, but I am also his strongest defender. He does the same for me. What we say about our spouse to others and how we react to others when they talk about our spouse is critical.

I remember years ago hearing about a crown being something that sets a person apart as special. Proverbs 12:4 says that a wife is her husband's crown. This means that the words I use to describe my husband or to tell a story about him paints a picture in the listener's mind. I can honor my husband or dishonor him by my words, especially in front of our children. Being intentional in marriage leads us to paint honoring mind-pictures about our spouse when speaking about them to others.

When friends get together and start complaining about their husbands or wives, this is dishonoring and most definitely not investing in the marriage relationship. There are some things that should never be said to others and remain only in the sacred trust of the marriage relationship. A rule of thumb I use is this: if Steve was present, would he mind me sharing this about him? The truth is, if we're not intentionally building our marriage up, we may be tearing it down by our unwholesome words.

Steve—My wife is more verbal than I am. This is not uncommon in marriage. In general, women tend to use more words than men on a daily basis. But for both of us the words that we speak come from the thoughts and feelings we have buried in our hearts. Jesus put it like this: *"A good man brings good things out of the good stored up in his heart, and an evil man brings evil things out of the evil stored up in his heart. For the mouth speaks what the heart is full of"* (Luke 6:45).

This means if I store up negative and hurtful things in my mind about Pam, I will ultimately speak negative and hurtful things to her. Thus, if I want to be intentional about speaking words of life to Pam, then I must plant in my mind healthy life-giving thoughts about her. Jesus says what I think in my mind will eventually come out in my words.

For some this may mean uprooting bitterness and other kinds of disappointment towards their spouse. Negative thoughts and feelings must be uprooted and healed before they can be replaced with positive thoughts and feelings.

However, in my case, this has rarely been necessary. For the most part, Pam has modeled Jesus' love and grace as much as anyone I've ever met. In fact, not long ago I was asked in a survey to identify my most influential spiritual mentor at this stage of my life. I said it was Pam. She has taught me more about Jesus than anyone!

But, nevertheless, if I am not intentional about forgiving and releasing hurts and disappointments, these irritants can cloud my thinking about Pam...just like anyone else. If I dwell too long on a critical comment, I can begin looking at my glass half empty rather than half full. This is why praying for Pam has been so helpful to keep my thoughts and feelings positive. When I pray for Pam, I ask for God's blessing upon her. I pray for her protection. I seek God's fullest and richest life for her. I do this daily. And as I pray for Pam, it positively shapes what I think about her and how I feel about her.

The Apostle Paul summarizes like this:

> *"Finally, brothers and sisters, whatever is true, whatever is noble, whatever is right, whatever is pure, whatever is lovely, whatever is admirable, if anything is excellent or praiseworthy, think about such things"* (Philippians 4:8).

The more I intentionally practice this with Pam, the more frequently I speak words of life to her. Almost every day I tell her how beautiful she is, what a great leader she is and how much I love her. This is a hugely important part of being intentional in our marriage because our words matter.

Be Intentional About Creating Memories

Pam—The best marriages intentionally create memories with some sizzle. However, for Steve and I being in ministry our entire adult lives has meant many lean times when there wasn't money for extravagant dates. To address this challenge sometimes we would switch off: one week I would plan the date, and the next week Steve would plan something. These experiences were always affordable, such as packing a dinner and two beach chairs, and driving down to the edge of the river to picnic. Other times we would go for walks and stop for a cup of tea or an ice-cream cone. Sometimes we would go for a drive and just talk in the car. No matter what the outing, creating memories was always our goal.

As the years have passed (and paying college bills is no longer in our budget), we now have more discretionary income. Not long ago for our anniversary, I surprised Steve with a jet boat ride in the San Francisco Bay. I had a budget, and a 30-minute ride in a jet boat fit the bill.

But the greatest part of the gift was that it was totally out of my comfort zone and completely out of character for me. Steve knew that merely getting into the jet boat was a sacrifice for me and it created a memory that we enjoyed for much longer than the 30 minutes of the ride. We laughed about it for months! Creating marriage memories is an incredibly significant investment. I want to caution you not to get so caught up doing the everyday stuff of life that you miss planning a surprise every once in a while.

There isn't a husband on earth that wouldn't thrill at his wife kidnapping him with a surprise overnight at a hotel. But the wife has to plan, think ahead, find childcare and arrange the details of the getaway. Husbands can do the same for their wives. The surprise factor puts sizzle into the relationship! These times are intentional investments that keep our marriage fresh, alive and fun.

A few years ago, I surprised Steve on a Friday night by telling him I was taking him out to dinner. When we got out of the car in the parking garage, I opened the trunk revealing a packed suitcase for an overnight at the hotel. I wish I had a picture of the expression on his face. It was worth a million words. He was completely blown away!

But, then, one of the times he shocked me was on our 27th anniversary. We had been talking for weeks that since we were married on August 27th, our 27th anniversary would be our "golden anniversary." I got this idea from those who celebrate their "golden birthday"—when the year corresponds with the day they were born. Since I was born May 1st and Steve was born August 6th, we were too young to have a "golden birthday" celebration. So, this was my reasoning for having a "golden anniversary." Steve swallowed it "hook, line and sinker" and he hit the ball out of the park with a surprise.

He picked me up from work, and we headed south on Highway 395. I was thinking, "Ok, maybe we're going to stay in Carson City." But we drove past Carson City and kept going. "Ok, maybe we'll stay in Bridgeport." But we kept going. Then when we turned west at Lee Vining, I knew with all certainty that the only place we could go was Yosemite National Park. Yosemite is very special to me because I spent many summer vacations there as a child. But then Steve pulls over and stops, takes out a CD, puts it in the player and plays "our song." It was a John Denver song called "Follow Me" that played on our eight-track cassette player decades earlier the first time Steve went to Yosemite with my family.

The last verse says,

> "I'd like to spend my life with you, show you things I've seen, places where I'm going, places where I've been. To have you there beside me and never be alone, and all the time that you're with me, we will be at home."

It was at that moment in the song in 1976, many years earlier, that I knew in my heart that Steve loved me.

Needless to say, I cried. We stayed at the Awahanee Hotel in the most expensive room we've ever paid for. (Steve still has not told me what it cost.) We ate dinner at the same honeymoon table where we had celebrated our 10th anniversary. Although Steve had reservations for that same table, it was not available when we arrived at the restaurant. But my husband insisted we wait. And wait we did—for over an hour.

But it was well worth it. The "honeymoon table" is situated in front of a large window looking out over a meadow surrounded by pines. What a beautiful surprise. What an extraordinary investment in "us!"

Intentionally creating sizzling memories can also be done at home after the kids are in bed. This was one reason we always put our children to bed early. We made sure we had time for "us." And whenever the kids would stay overnight with friends or with extended family, Steve and I had loads of fun. Maybe it was a quiet dinner or a lingering romantic conversation in front of the fireplace...one way or another we have intentionally created memories along the way.

Steve—Intentionally creating memories also includes planning rich and meaningful sexual experiences as a married couple. It may come as a surprise to some, but a terrific sex life does not happen accidentally. Both husband and wife need to be intentional for this vital part of marriage to thrive. Great sex takes time and energy. Yet scores of married people have told me that time and energy is precisely what they lack most. Unfortunately, this will often result in a lackluster sex life. The marriage sizzle of the early years wanes to a feeble whimper. In my opinion, this is tragic and completely unnecessary.

To prevent this from happening, Pam and I intentionally plan for times of sexual intimacy. We both know what's on each other's calendars and, when we see an evening that is open, we talk about its possibilities. We communicate ahead of time that we're looking forward to being together. We are both intentional about this. Planning ahead in this way helps us to be on the same wavelength through the day...

and it also helps me to keep a guard over my tongue so I don't say something stupid that might spoil everything!

Creating memorable sexual experiences involves forethought and creativity. Like most couples, there have been seasons where Pam and I allowed our sex life to become dull and overly predictable. But in this season of our marriage, we have become far more adventurous and fun. I believe that God created sex to be one of the most fulfilling and electrifying dimensions of marriage—but this will not happen accidentally. It will only happen if a married couple intentionally creates memories in this arena.

Be Intentional About Ministering to Your Spouse

Pam—Being intentional in marriage also means intentionally ministering to each other. If I have a soapbox, it is this: If we are married, then God has given us a vital ministry that no one else has on this earth—this is our ministry to our spouse. When we consider our spouse as our first and most important ministry, this opens the door for the marriage relationship to flourish. When I say "ministry" I mean that God brings a husband and wife together for each of them to mutually love, help, pray for, support, encourage and nurture each other.

What does this look like? Well, when I look at my God-given calling to "minister" to Steve, I end up serving him with joy and not with resentment. This leads me to pray for God to show me how to best minister to him. God answers these prayers by giving me wonderful ideas to make life special for him, such as cooking tasty meals, lighting candles and making sure he has the food he likes in the refrigerator.

God also answers my prayers by helping me to understand when Steve needs time to rest and be quiet or when he needs a special touch of creative sex. The best part of this is when I physically "minister" to Steve in this way, not only is he happy, but I have fun too!

If I look at my marriage as my first and most important ministry, recognizing it as a personal ministry to Steve that no one else has, (a ministry that God himself has entrusted to me), it motivates me to be faithful to God and his unique calling on my life.

When a married couple ministers to each other with this attitude there is less selfishness in the relationship. Resentment sets in when I focus on myself and I begin feeling like Steve never does anything for "me." But when I take my eyes off myself and look for God-directed ways to minister to Steve—look out! This is the best way to live life! The Bible is clear about this: *"He who seeks to save his life will lose it. But he who loses his life for me and for the gospel will save it"* (Mark 8:35).

This is true for both wives and husbands. Whenever Steve cleans up the kitchen after a meal, whenever he surprises me with a washed car and a full tank of gas, whenever he serves me (which he often does), it blesses my heart. Whenever he listens to me and tries to understand my feelings, my love for him grows deeper. This is what it means to minister to each other intentionally. It is a holy calling that God has given to every spouse—a unique calling no one else has. This is supremely important!

Ministering to each other occasionally means doing things for your spouse that they may not like doing for themselves. For instance, Steve doesn't like to make travel arrangements, so I do that for us. He appreciates not getting bogged down in the details. On the other hand, emptying the dishwasher isn't my favorite chore. Because my husband knows this, he empties it every opportunity he can—and I know he is doing it for me. And whenever I do have to empty the dishwasher, I am thankful I don't have to do it often. (I also know that if Steve were home, he'd be doing it to serve me.) I can't tell you how many couples have never thought of their marriage as a ministry to be able to serve that one special person God has given them.

The Five Love Languages by Gary Chapman has been helpful. The book helped me to see that Steve's love language is acts of service. Quite honestly, there have been times Steve did things for me that I didn't even notice. For years I didn't appreciate him washing my car. I didn't even know it was dirty! But when I realized that he was saying "I love you" by washing my car, I started noticing, and now I appreciate it.

I also have had to look intentionally for acts of service I can do for him to make him feel loved. This doesn't come naturally to me because it's not my love language—but it is Steve's. I also appreciate that even though Steve may not feel like sitting down and listening and talking, he knows that words are my love language—and he does it joyfully. He knows that when I have quality time in conversation, I feel deeply loved. And because Steve wants to minister to me in my love language, he takes the time and exerts the effort to do it.

If we see our marriage relationship as an opportunity to minister to the most special person in our life, then we will pray for the Holy Spirit's power to minister through us. And I know it is especially tough with young kids. The squeaky wheel gets the grease, and young children are good at being little squeakers! It is easy to tend to them and forget that our spouse has needs too. Just because they may not be "squeaking," doesn't mean that our spouse's needs are any less real.

When children come along, husbands especially need to step up to the plate to minister to their brides by making sure their wives have time to feed their own souls. I feel one of the best ways a husband can minister to his wife is to make sure she has time to refresh herself. Everyone is different. Some are refreshed being with girlfriends, others by going out by themselves. But all of us need to spend time in the Word of God and prayer. However, finding sufficient time to do this becomes daunting for mothers with young children and for wives who work outside the home.

Husbands need to have a special sensitivity to this challenge. This may mean husbands taking over in the early morning or in the evening so the wife can have time alone with God. When our children were younger, all of us had our "quiet time" right after lunch. The little ones took a nap and the older children quietly read on their beds. This gave me time alone to read my Bible and pray. My kids knew what I was doing and what was expected of them, and it worked for several years. Later, when the kids were all in school, time for my spiritual nourishment became more accessible. But Steve made sure that I was feeding my soul because he understood that I was his most important ministry.

Steve—I've already mentioned praying daily for Pam. Years ago a mentor told me that if God ever calls you to a ministry, he first calls you to pray for that ministry. With that in mind, I realize that my daily persistent prayers for Pam are indispensable. I understand the sacred responsibility I have to love Pam as Christ loved the church. I feel the weight of God's calling to present my wife before the Lord without stain or wrinkle or any other blemish. As I said earlier, in my opinion, Ephesians 5:25-33 is one of the most challenging passages in the Bible. To underscore what Pam has said—she is my most important ministry. And I will be held accountable for how I conduct myself. So will every husband. Gentlemen, we dare not take lightly our roles as husbands!

Needless to say, intentionally ministering to Pam involves more than prayer. It also means providing for her physical well-being. We have never been wealthy. But whenever it comes to allocation decisions, my wife always comes first.

(When the children lived at home, Pam and I agreed to put them first. But now that our kids are gone, I take care of Pam first.) Her needs always trump mine. And I don't do that begrudgingly. This is part of what it means to love my wife as Christ loved the church. Jesus died for the church. As I walk this out, it pales in comparison to put buying Pam's contact lens above me getting a new shirt. The comparison is absurd. God calls me to die for Pam if necessary!

Another way I minister to Pam is to empower her to become all that God designed her to be. My role is not to shackle her or hold her back. Quite to the contrary, as her husband, my role is to help Pam fulfill her greatest potential as a child of God. This has meant encouraging her to step out in faith and do things she never dreamed she could do—like living overseas, speaking to large crowds, leading robust ministries and even writing a book. The primary reason these things have happened is because I have intentionally made Pam my most important ministry.

Be Intentional About Saying "No!"

Pam—Another key to being intentional in marriage is learning to say "no." We have learned this the hard way many times over. In our first year in seminary, we decided we should have a dog. We also decided it should be a puppy so we could train it to be a wonderful and obedient dog. Did I say we were naïve? Well, we found an ad for free puppies in Chicago and decided to take the trip from the Chevrolet car dealer where we had just picked up our brand new Chevy Chevette.

Even though it had less than 10,000 miles, the Fiat we owned at the time "died" that first Midwest winter. (We wondered if it had been made in southern Italy because it was certainly not built for the cold weather in Illinois.) Why did we buy a Chevette? Because we could walk to the Chevy dealer down the street from our house! The day we bought the new car, we literally prayed that our Fiat would make it to the dealer so we could use it as a trade-in.

So, with our brand new car, smelling like a new car, we drove into downtown Chicago with snow piled high from a record-breaking snowstorm. We found the apartment, and after being invited in, and trying to not step on the dozens of cats and other animals that covered the floors, we were led to a golden lab with several darling puppies. The breeder informed us that the father was a Malamute. We chose the prettiest female puppy, wrapped her up in a towel and took her home. Unfortunately, she was not good at traveling and threw up in our new car—which after a few hours had already lost the "new car" smell.

Because Steve was studying Greek in seminary, we named our dog Arena, which means "Peace" in Greek. (I wonder how many seminary students give their pets Greek names?) Arena was a beautiful dog. But being naïve we forgot about the fact that we were never home during the week, and our weekends were full of youth ministry activities.

This wasn't a good scenario to train a puppy! I remember one time coming home from work to find every potted plant in the house dug up and dirt strewn everywhere. Another day Arena broke down the barricade that was supposed to keep her in the kitchen, and she tore up one of our wedding picture albums.

Lesson learned: Puppies need owners who have time to care for them. God also used those difficulties to begin teaching Steve and me that we have limits. We will never have the time and energy to do everything we might desire. Not surprisingly, it would take years for this lesson to sink in fully. We were still young and invincible.

But, in his sovereignty, God began showing us early in our marriage that we only had so much time and energy. Choosing to live within those God-given limits is critical for a marriage to thrive. Every time we have pressed ourselves too far, our marriage has suffered.

This became even more acute once our first-born child, Rachel, came along. Our time as a couple became even more limited. I quit working at the seminary to be home with Rachel and Steve started working nights at UPS, along with going to school full-time in the day and doing student ministry on the weekends.

During that intense season, we had precious little time together. God was gracious (as usual), and our marriage survived. But it would take many more hard lessons before we finally learned that it's okay for us to say "no" to some things in order to say "yes" to the things that enable us to intentionally invest in our marriage.

Steve—One very important reason to say "no" to over-commitment and harried scheduling is to allow enough margin in your marriage for rest and replenishment. The longer I live, the more convinced I am that adequate rest is essential for us to thrive as human beings—and it's even more vital for a marriage to sizzle. Yet, like many important things in life, rest will generally not happen unless we are intentional. God designed us to live with weekly rhythms of rest—it's called the Sabbath. But, sadly, the principle of Sabbath rest may be the most frequently ignored principle in the Bible.

This is to our detriment as individuals and as married couples. I'm sure I'm not the only one who becomes grumpy and impatient when I'm overly tired. And I'm also sure that I'm not the only one to have said unkind things to my spouse in those seasons of excessive fatigue.

Now, it may seem too obvious, but one of the best ways to prevent unnecessary conflict with your spouse is to get adequate rest. Like most people, when I'm rested and refreshed small irritants role easily off my back. But when I am overly tired things can get messy very quickly.

This is why Pam and I have become very intentional about making sure we have adequate rhythms of rest and refreshment. This may not be for every couple, but we generally go to bed together quite early. It's rare when we stay up later than 9:00 PM. We don't have a television in our bedroom because it's our sanctuary to communicate and connect with each other. Occasionally we'll watch TV in the living room, but we prefer, by far, just to talk together with soft music in the background.

One very important side benefit from getting adequate

rest is how it puts sizzle into our sex life. As I said earlier, great sex takes time and energy. But when a married couple is continuously tired, sex can be reduced to a mechanical activity which serves merely to meet pent-up biological needs. This is a far cry from God's design. God created sex to be an incredible celebration of marital love between husband and wife! We'll talk more about it in the next two chapters.

This raises an important question: what do you need to say "no" to in your life in order to be more intentional about getting adequate rest and refreshment?

Be Intentional About Your Calendar and Budget

Pam—It takes careful planning to be intentional in the marriage relationship. There are endless wonderful things to do with other people. Steve and I have a regular stream of invitations to do fun things and hang out with people we enjoy. This is all good. But unless we plan ahead and carefully consider our week, our month and our year's schedule, the time we need together as a couple gets shoved aside as we make ourselves overly available to others. As a result, to keep our marriage relationship sizzling we have learned we need to be the masters of our schedules.

To do this wisely, we have found it essential to check with each other's calendar before saying yes to an invitation. If we look at our week's schedule and see there are only one or two nights free (which means all the other nights are full), that means our week is already too full, and we will decline the invitation. We do this to keep a sustainable pace and to guard our time alone together.

Somewhere, somehow, in our society, some people have decided that busier is better. Some families have their kids in every sport imaginable, and they run consistently at full steam. When this happens, often one of the first things to suffer is sizzle in the marriage relationship.

Tim Kimmel in his book *Little House on the Freeway* puts it like this: "I've watched the speed at which we live our lives shift from second gear into overdrive. But since few people these days have driven a stick shift, how about this analogy? We're running at Mach 2 with our hair on fire!" That says it so well.

Families are busier and busier doing everything they can to give their children every opportunity available. But one of the most important things children need is for mom and dad to have a flourishing relationship. If time and attention are not invested in the marriage, it will not grow and flourish. Instead, it will dry up and blow away. The garden of the marriage relationship has to be tended to stay strong. It may sound simple, but it's profoundly true: being intentional in marriage means taking control of the calendar.

Steve—It also means taking control of the budget. For a couple to intentionally invest in their marriage requires at least a minimal allocation of resources toward the marriage. Pam already mentioned that we've had many financially lean times as a result of being in full-time ministry our entire married lives. But that rarely stopped us from socking away at least a few dollars for a date at Starbucks, or to buy an ice cream cone together.

Now that we enjoy a bit more financial stability, we carefully budget for our periodic "get-away" trips. Once again, no one can have it all. It's long been said that you can only spend a dollar once. Every allocation decision means you are deciding not to spend that dollar somewhere else. Over the years I have observed that people spend money on what they want. No matter how modest the income, it seems if people want to have the latest cell phone or electric gadget, they find the money to purchase those things.

That being said, Pam and I have intentionally decided to budget money to invest in our marriage. In any given season this may mean that we don't wear the latest fashions or have the most recent iPhones or eat out as often as others do. Like you, we have financial limits. So we choose to use most of our discretionary money to invest in our relationship. Being intentional for us also means leveraging the budget to build sizzle into our marriage.

In view of everything we've said in this chapter, Pam and I hope you take the time to read this more than once—and that you do it slowly. It's chalk-a-block full of practical suggestions. God created an incredible gift with marriage. But it takes intentionality to experience a marriage that truly sizzles.

Chapter Seven

Section #7
Pray Naked

Pam—It's okay, admit it! This is the secret you've been waiting for! It is probably the most famous thing Steve has ever said from the pulpit. A few years ago, we were both teaching a series on marriage in our church. Steve mentioned that in his experience as a pastor, he has observed that most married men want to have more sex and most wives want their husbands to be more spiritual.

So he suggested that married couples pray naked together. That way the wife is happy because her husband is doing something spiritual with her. And the husband is happy because, as they say, one thing often leads to another. Our congregation quoted Steve for months! Some folks even threatened to get t-shirts that said: "I Pray Naked!" It was hilarious!

Now, frankly, when Steve first mentioned it, I was a bit embarrassed that he had revealed one of the secrets to our sizzling marriage. But the more I see the critical need for healing and vibrancy and passionate life-giving sex in marriages, the happier I am sharing "our little secret."

Praying naked is one of the secrets Steve and I have discovered to keep our marriage sizzling. But I remind you that this cannot be taken in isolation from everything else we've said. There's a reason we've placed this chapter after we've discussed other things, such as putting Christ first in your marriage and selflessly serving each other.

Praying naked is foreplay for the main event. Just like the husband and wife kissing and caressing each other are essential physical foreplay to sexual intercourse, so is the spiritual and emotional oneness that is created by praying naked. If you want your marriage to sizzle, keep reading!

Steve—*"The two become one flesh"* (Genesis 2:24). I've performed hundreds of weddings, and I almost always include these words. Most people assume *"one flesh"* has to do strictly with the husband and wife becoming one in a sexual sense. But that is only part of what it means.

For two people to become one flesh involves much more than merely sexual intercourse—sexual intercourse can happen in a moment. But true intimacy, becoming genuinely one flesh, takes a lifetime. Becoming one flesh in the fullest sense takes years of living together, praying together, working together, crying together, hurting together, supporting together, selflessly laying down our lives, releasing anger, endlessly forgiving and much more.

Pam and I believe that God has more for marriage than most people realize. God designed marriage so that a man and a woman could become *"one flesh"* in the deepest possible sense. We call this a marriage that sizzles!

I find it interesting that after God created the world, he had Adam name the animals. Each of the animals had a mate...except Adam. It was at that point that God created the woman. *"But for Adam, no suitable helper was found. So the LORD God caused the man to fall into a deep sleep; and while he was sleeping, he took one of the man's ribs and then closed up the place with flesh"* (Genesis 2:20-21).

God fashioned the woman from the man's rib. Frequently during wedding ceremonies, I explain that Eve was not taken from Adam's head to rule over him, nor was she taken from his feet to be stepped on by him. The woman was taken from the man's rib because she was designed to be his partner. The term *"suitable helper"* means counterpart. The woman was designed by God to complement the man just as the man was designed to complement the woman. The sum of both together, as a married couple, becomes something far greater than either could be alone.

Genesis 2:24-25 continues with foundational teaching on marriage. *"That is why a man leaves his father and mother and is united to his wife, and they become one flesh. Adam and his wife were both naked, and they felt no shame."*

Undergirding this sweeping statement about marriage is God's vision for two people—husband and wife—to increasingly experience spiritual and emotional oneness. Then, as an outgrowth of their oneness of soul, the married couple celebrates with sexual intercourse. Using the words of Genesis 2:24, they become one flesh.

Now, this is vital not to miss. The celebration of sexual intimacy was never designed by God to stand alone as merely a physical act. But when a husband and wife continue to draw together spiritually and emotionally, then sexual intercourse becomes much more meaningful and much more sizzling!

Pam and I have discovered that the best sex has come after years of growing together as soul mates. This is because God created sex to be more than merely "the act of marriage." Sex is designed by God to express the overflow of the soul connection between a husband and wife. This is why sex becomes more enjoyable as the husband and wife grow closer together spiritually and emotionally.

Leaving and Cleaving

For this to happen, the text is clear that the man must leave his father and mother, and be united to his wife. The King James Version says the man is "to cleave" to his wife. To cleave is an old word and it is a strong word. It means to cling tightly. Think of how the fingers on both your hands can intertwine and become knit together. That's a picture of what it means to cleave together as husband and wife.

God is telling us that in marriage there must be a leaving and cleaving. God knew that for a marriage to be all that he intended, both the husband and wife must leave their mother and father and cleave to each other. One reason some marriages don't thrive is because there has never been a leaving by either the husband or the wife. When this happens, they cannot cleave to their spouse in the way God intends because they are still emotionally cleaving to their parents or to someone else. So there must be a leaving before there can be a cleaving.

This is why, as parents, we took a step back when our three girls got married. The girls not only needed to leave our home, but they also needed to leave Pam and I, as their parents, so that they could cleave to their new husbands. Our relationship with our girls had to change for them to have a healthy relationship with their husbands.

Now, in truth, there were times that we stepped over the line and gave more advice than the girls wanted or needed. Admittedly, there were other times when the girls wanted more of a relationship with us than we offered. But when each of them got married, it was a new "dance" step that we all had to learn.

When Pam and I were first married, her mother called her every morning after I left for work. When I found out about this a few months into our marriage, it did not sit well with me. I felt like the daily calls were an intrusion into our marriage space. Marriage was new for us, and I needed to know that I came first in Pam's life.

As I look back, I can see more clearly how immature I was acting. But, none the less, Pam asked her mother not to call every day. She suggested calling a couple of times a week to give us more space to be husband and wife. Thankfully, Pam's mom respected our request. This was a watershed moment in Pam's relationship with her mom, and in our marriage as well. From that day onward, I never wondered if I was the most important human relationship in Pam's life.

Genesis 2:25 says, *"Adam and his wife were both naked, and they felt no shame."* This is much more than merely being physically naked. God designed marriage to be a relationship with complete oneness. In marriage, the husband and wife can grow to become one on at least three levels: spiritually, emotionally and physically. When all three happen, it leads to a sizzling marriage!

Spiritual Oneness

Pam—Spiritual oneness is when the husband and wife both grow individually as Christ followers and, at the same time, they are also growing together as a couple in their relationship with the Lord. Spiritual oneness is essential for a truly sizzling marriage. We mentioned at the beginning of this book that nothing we have written about marriage will make sense apart from a life deeply rooted in Christ.

A few years back, Steve brought out the box of letters that we wrote to each other while we were dating. He had spent eight months in Bible school in Sweden, and during that season we wrote prolifically to each other. As we read through the letters, we both were struck by how much passion we had for the Lord. Our greatest goal in life was to love Jesus with all our heart, soul, mind and strength and to serve him faithfully. Now, I know that doesn't happen in every relationship, but at least in our case, we started out with Jesus at the center. Jesus was everything for us—and he still is!

So, how can we cultivate spiritual oneness? Francis and Lisa Chan, in their book, *You and Me Forever: Marriage in Light of Eternity,* suggest that the most important thing we can do for our marriage is for each of us to seek the Lord individually. God wants to be the highest priority in our life—he wants to be our first love. We must be right with God first before we can experience true spiritual oneness with our spouse.

Praying for each other is another way we cultivate spiritual oneness. This is important because as we pray for each other, we are changed. Sometimes what happens in us as we pray is even more important than what we pray will happen in our spouse. In addition, as we pray we allow the Holy Spirit do the work in our spouse, instead of trying to make it happen ourselves.

I love how Frank Laubach, in *Letters by a Modern Mystic,* talks about prayer in marriage.

"Sweethearts who have been wise enough to share their love with God have found it incomparably more wonderful. God is love. He is in deepest sympathy with every fond whisper and look. Husbands and wives, too, give rapturous testimony of homes transformed by praying silently when together. In some cases where they had begun to give each other 'nerves,' they have found, after playing this game (thinking of God one second of every minute) when they are alone together by day or by night, that their love grew strangely fresh, rich, beautiful, 'like a honeymoon.'

"God is the maker of all true marriages, and he gives his highest joy to a man and wife who share their love for each other with him when they are together looking into one another's eyes. Married love becomes infinitely more wonderful when Christ is the bond every minute, and it grows sweet as the years go by to the very last day."

When I look at Steve, I thank the Lord for the joy of being his wife and for the blessings I experience each day by his side. Sometimes, as I look at him, I will silently ask God to encourage him and pour out his love on him.

When I am feeling frustrated with Steve, or hurt by his words, I try to take that hurt and frustration immediately to Jesus. "Okay, Jesus, you've got to help me with this! I surrender my feelings to you. I know my husband is tired or under pressure right now. Help me to respond to him with patience and love. I don't want to get defensive." When I do this, things usually settle down, and I don't focus on myself.

This is vital because whenever I focus on myself, I end up getting defensive or angry, and my words come out as a selfish reaction rather than loving and kind.

The normal frustrations of everyday life seem less apparent when my focus is on Jesus. This is why prayer is so important. If I am going to be the wife that God wants me to be, and the wife that my husband needs, then it is critical that I keep my focus on Jesus—the One that sustains me, gives me strength and who will never disappoint me. He alone is the One True God. This happens through prayer.

If you are feeling less than satisfied with your marriage, prayer is the place you start. When you bring your marriage before the Lord, you are inviting the King of kings and the Lord of lords to do the work that you cannot do. You are inviting supernatural power from above, to change both of your hearts and minds, to fill both of you with his love, and to give you both the wisdom to navigate your differences.

Many times we leave prayer as a last resort. Instead, it should be the first and foremost gift that we leverage in our marriage. Ask your spouse how you can pray for him or her—and then pray. Keep a prayer notebook where you write down your requests, and keep track of God's answers. It will grow your faith, and it will grow your marriage until it sizzles.

We can all see the things that need to be changed in our spouse. Pointing those out bluntly usually doesn't help. But we have a wonderful Lord that hears our prayers, and more change can happen through prayer than we might imagine. I remember years ago when I realized that, other than my prayer-warrior parents, no one else was consistently praying for Steve. I recall the feeling of being weighted down by the realization that if I didn't pray consistently for my husband, then I would be seriously letting him down as his wife. From that point on, I have been committed to praying for him.

For over 30 years I have kept a prayer notebook which I update in January every year. I have a photo of the person I am praying for on each page with a list of specific requests. My prayer requests for Steve are noted, and answers are written in red ink with the date. As the year progresses, I am amazed at the red ink on that page from the answered prayers. Seeing those answers mount up inspires me to press on and pray more. The prayer requests are specific. One may be for a difficult lunch meeting Steve has or a situation with a disgruntled church member. Some prayer requests are on-going, such as praying for wisdom and insight, sermon preparation, leadership inspiration, and leading our church staff.

One of my most important roles as Steve's wife, if not the most crucial, is to pray for him. I also bring my prayer requests to Steve and ask him to pray for those things. Many times he already knows, and he's already praying. It blesses me to know that my husband is aware of my needs and he is taking them to the Lord on my behalf.

Praying together as a couple is also vital for spiritual oneness. This is where praying naked can play an essential role in marriage. And I am very serious about this! God wants married couples to seek him together, and also to have passionate and frequent sex. These two gifts are mysteriously and wonderfully woven together in a marriage that sizzles.

Steve—But before we go any further, we want to address what may be the elephant in the room. Perhaps the thought of praying naked with your spouse is repulsive to you. As a result, hearing us talk about this may bring up all kinds of negative feelings. This may be especially true for those who have been abused in the past. Tragically, an alarming number of people have been sexually abused in one form or another and this can leave deep soul-scars.

Because of this, Pam and I want to urge those who may suffer from flashbacks or unresolved wounds due to sexual abuse to get professional help to heal. We do not have the training or skills to address those issues. We can only say that marriage, as God designed it, can become one of the most intimate of all human relationships. Because of this, we hope you desire all that God has for you in your marriage.

Thus, if you have suffered from sexual abuse in the past, we strongly suggest you get the professional help you may need. We urge this because we want you to enjoy your spouse in every way, and we want you to be free from the past shadows that might cloud your marriage. We believe that God can heal our past. And many times God uses Christian marriage and family counselors in this process.

We'd like to share a simple illustration. Bill Denney is a good friend and long-time marriage and family therapist. He shared that, in his experience, many couples that have sex together before marriage are unable to touch each other without that touch being understood as sexual. As a result, Bill often asks these couples to refrain from having sex for a week or so in order to learn to touch each other without sex being the goal. He said this simple "therapy" has helped many couples to give and receive gentle touches to communicate "I love you" and "I know you are there" rather than being misunderstood as sexual foreplay.

Our desire is to encourage all married couples to experience a marriage that sizzles. We realize that every couple is different. But once we are free from lingering past shadows, praying naked in marriage can be very meaningful for Christian couples.

Now, to find time to pray together naked requires intentionality. Many "normal" days in our home I rise early and leave before Pam is up. Those days are obviously not conducive to praying naked together. But we have a prime opportunity whenever I have a day off, or our schedule allows more leisure time in the morning.

To be completely honest, praying naked is a vital part of our experience when we get away alone as a couple. "Normal life" may be accelerated and not allow much time to lollygag in bed. This is especially true if young children are at home. This is one reason Pam and I are so enamored with escaping alone as a couple. It frees us up from the rigors of our normal schedule to enjoy deeper connections with the Lord and with each other. Gentlemen, I hope this inspires you to find a way to get away for a few days with your bride!

P am—Another way to cultivate spiritual oneness is to be aware of our spouse's relationship with the Lord. Steve and I regularly ask each other, "What is God teaching you in your devotional time?" We share with each other what we are reading in God's Word. As we talk about the Lord together, we also have a better idea how to pray for each other.

I feel protected and cared for knowing that my husband is concerned with my spiritual life. I love sharing with him what I have been reading. I highlight and make notes in books that I read and share those things with Steve so we can discuss them. I have been known to pull out a list on post-it notes of things I have read in the Bible or in other books that I want to share with him.

Still another way to cultivate spiritual oneness is to serve the Lord together. When I see God using Steve, and when he sees the Lord using me, it gives us an opportunity to encourage each other. The reason I am almost always at church for our Saturday evening service is because Steve wants to hear my opinion about his message. This is one way that I spiritually encourage him.

You may think that because my husband is a pastor, serving together is something we "have to do." But even if Steve was not a pastor, I would serve by his side. Having common interests and activities is essential in marriage, but serving the living Christ together moves this to a whole new level. Living with spiritual purpose and meaning puts vitality into a marriage like nothing else!

On the other hand, Steve also knows how important my ministry is with our Women's Encounter, and he asks me about it regularly. Awhile back, he even drove the 60 miles to the Encounter on a Friday night so that he could sit in on one session...just to encourage me. Throughout our marriage we have served the Lord together and, usually, this has enhanced the spiritual oneness in our marriage.

Marriage Illustrates Life with Jesus

In several places in Scripture, notably Ephesians 5, God uses intimacy in marriage as an illustration of Christ's relationship with his church. The church, in this case, refers to those who are adopted into his forever family by faith in Christ. Steve and I have pondered this a great deal. How does our marriage reflect God's desire for an intimate relationship with us, his bride, the church?

With this question in mind, I have been struck by St. Teresa of Avila's writings. Teresa was a Carmelite nun who wrote between 1546 and 1582 in Spain. Contained within her writings are descriptions of prayer that bear evidence to her amazingly intimate relationship with the Lord. One of her most famous books is called *Interior Castle*.

In the book, Teresa describes praying and relates this experience:

> "It is like being suddenly encountered by a most fragrant perfume so that it is diffused through all the senses... I meagerly use this as a comparison in order to convey the excitement with which the soul is aroused in the presence of the Spouse and the intoxicating desire to enjoy him."

In Allison Peer's translation of *Interior Castle*, some of Teresa's descriptions of prayer border on descriptions of intimacy in marriage. Teresa of Avila is just one of many examples throughout church history of people who experienced deeply intimate communion with the Lord.

As we have reflected on this, in some mysterious way, Steve and I have come to believe that intimacy between a husband and wife can mirror the intimate communion that God invites us to experience with him.

Think about it. In Genesis 3, Adam and Eve walked and talked with God in the Garden of Eden. That must have been amazing! At first, the relationship between God and Adam and Eve was pristine. But then sin entered the scene and Adam and Eve decided to do things their way instead of trusting God. As a result, there was a tragic breakdown in humanity's relationship with God. However, because of the blood of Jesus, once again we can have the privilege of walking with God in intimate communion.

But what does this ongoing communion with God look like? Well, throughout Scripture we read about God's amazing love for us. He seeks us out. He has our name written on the palm of his hand. He rejoices over us with singing. We are the apple of his eye. We are his focus and delight.

In response to his lavish love for us, we call out to him the moment we wake up in the morning. After praising him for who he is and thanking him for what he has done for us, we ask for his Spirit to fill us that day. We express our desire to walk in step with his Spirit and to be aware of his presence. We ask for his wisdom, and we give him dominion over our day. We also ask him to search our hearts and to let us know where we have tried to do things our own way instead of his.

Throughout the day, we call upon him, asking him, for example, to be present in any conversation we're going to have, or for his help as we make a decision, or to come to the aid of those we love. We pray for wisdom for our children and grandchildren, as well as for their protection. Ideally, this communion continues throughout the day until we lay our heads down on our pillows and thank him for all he has done that day. We sleep in peace because he is with us and has control of our lives.

Okay, you say, "Come on! You do this every day?" And we will say, quite honestly, "No, not every day." But we sure try. It is our goal. However, in reality, there are parts of days when we don't even think about God. The ideal is to keep God fully in focus every day. But we are broken people—we get distracted or annoyed, or we take our eyes off him, and we try to do things our own way instead of his way.

Whenever this happens, after we realize it, we ask forgiveness and renew our commitment to keep our mind fixed on God, living for him and trusting him instead of continuing forward in our own strength.

Oneness in marriage is similar. In the same way that God wants us to connect with him regularly, marriages that sizzle connect together regularly. For example, when Steve and I wake up on a leisurely morning, we are usually content to be next to the one we have spent years getting to know. The peace and completeness we feel are due to the trust, the openness, and the investment we have made in our relationship. When I rest my head on Steve's chest, and we pray together naked, I often think, "Oh Lord, I feel perfect peace. This is how you want me to feel when I am with you."

Selflessness is the doorway to this depth of oneness, both with Jesus and with our spouse. Only when we renounce ourselves and wholeheartedly submit to God will we hear him, feel him, enjoy him and walk closely with him. Basically, we have to get out of the way.

The same is true in marriage. As long as it is all about me, true oneness in marriage breaks down. This is because I can't see beyond the end of my own nose to understand what my husband is feeling or thinking. Whenever it's "all about me" I become defensive for myself and my perspective is clouded because I am self-absorbed. The same is true with Steve. Repentance and forgiveness is the only way to get back on track. This is important because oneness in marriage grows deeper especially when both husband and wife have clean hearts.

To have a sizzling marriage, we have to take the time to connect. This doesn't mean here and there conversations about when to pick up Johnny from soccer practice or to get more milk at the corner market. Connecting means communicating soul to soul. It takes time, it takes intentionality, and it takes effort.

Remember when you were dating and you couldn't wait to see each other? Sometimes those feelings dissipate over time. If that has been your experience, I encourage you to pray for renewed feelings toward your spouse. Husbands, if you do not look forward to coming home to your sweetheart, I urge you to pray for God to give you a new longing to be with your bride. Wives, if you do not eagerly look forward to your man coming home, I also urge you to pray for God to renew your desire to be with him.

I look forward to hearing about my husband's day when he gets home. I have been praying for specific meetings and other concerns of his. I also look forward to pleasing him with a nice dinner, and I want to look refreshed and as pretty as I can. If Steve is my first ministry, and I believe he is, then I want to look forward to ministering to him. Men are not complicated. Little things we do as wives can go a long way to making our man happy. We will talk in more detail about that in the next chapter!

Another way that marriage reflects our relationship with Christ is that the more we know each other as husband and wife the deeper our love grows. This is similar to our relationship to Christ. The more we know about God, the more time we spend with him, the more we desire to be in his presence, the more we will grow to love him. The more we are aware of God's presence, the more we want to be in his presence.

How do we get to know Christ in a deeper and more vital way? We spend time with him. We take time to be alone with him and listen to him. We plan extended devotional times where we can drink him in and listen to him. These times of contemplation are necessary to know Christ in a deeper way. Quiet, silence, relaxed, unhurried blocks of time feed our souls with a deeper knowledge of Christ. When Steve and I get away to rest, we have extended times of silence to nurture our intimacy with the Lord.

Marriage mirrors this intimacy with Christ. When I sleep next to Steve, I can hear him breathe, and my knee, or foot, or arm, or hand reaches out to touch him to feel him near. I love sleeping while having physical contact of some sort to feel that Steve is there. It is similar to walking with Christ knowing without a shadow of doubt that he is with us.

Thus, there are many ways that the marriage relationship reflects our relationship with Jesus. This is why spiritual oneness is pivotal to a sizzling marriage. One of the best ways to improve a marriage is by growing spiritually. Generally speaking, the more the life of Jesus individually consumes a husband and wife, the more selfless and loving they become, which then leads to sizzling results within their marriage relationship.

Emotional Oneness

Steve—Emotional oneness happens when the husband and wife begin to peel the layers off the onion skin and, bit by bit, they begin to be more and more vulnerable with each other. This doesn't happen overnight, and frankly, it doesn't happen in every marriage. Sadly, some marriages never seem to experience this. Pam and I believe that emotional oneness is what God wants for every marriage, and we believe that every married couple can experience this if they're intentional.

A friend, who has been a marriage counselor for many decades, told us about his parent's marriage. His parents were committed to each other. They did the "right things." They both were Christ followers. But there was little emotional connection.

Unfortunately, he said this is what many couples settle for. Pam and I have discovered that the kind of sizzling physical oneness we are talking about only comes after a husband and wife develop a significant sense of emotional oneness.

We dedicated an entire chapter to lingering conversations. These can help create emotional oneness. Lingering conversations are the times when Pam and I sit and chat for hours. They don't happen every week, but a couple of times a month Pam and I find ourselves drifting into what we've come to call lingering conversations when we open up to each other in profound ways.

This takes a block of uninterrupted time. Unfortunately, some married couples don't invest this time. They are always in a hurry. Because of this, I think that excessive busyness is one of the chief enemies of marriage. By its very nature, you can't rush a lingering conversation. And you can't manufacture them either. They just happen every once in a while if we allow time and space for them.

Fatigue is another factor that keeps emotional oneness from happening. Couples are often too tired to open up. This is one reason Pam and I guard our calendar so fiercely. We've said for years that no one can "have it all." Something has to give. And if we want to experience emotional oneness in marriage, then we dare not live in a constant state of fatigue. Don't be afraid to take naps or get to bed early. Look at your week and month before scheduling more activities and engagements.

Another key to emotional oneness is asking insightful open-ended questions. A great resource is the book *201 Great Questions for Married Couples* by Jerry Jones. We've used resources like this many times. And do you know what? We've been married for more than 40 years, and we are still discovering new things about each other. It's been an extraordinary journey. I have always had a knack for asking good questions. When we go out with people we don't know, we learn about them and through questions, we dig deeper into their lives. It's much more fun than talking about the weather. Pam has been growing in this area. She is now much more intentional about asking creative questions in conversations with others and with me.

Simple habits can also help a married couple to emotionally connect. Pam and I regularly tell each other how much we enjoy being together and how thankful we are for each other. During the day, we may call each other to check in or text to say that we are thinking about the other.

Pam makes it a point to thank me for all the things I do around the house. Similarly, when I thank Pam for doing the laundry or ironing, she feels appreciated knowing that I value what she does. A thankful word goes a long way. Trying to out-serve each other can be fun! If Pam knows that bringing in the trash cans from the curb into the backyard will bless me, then she does it just to bless me. Doing simple things like these help us to connect emotionally as a married couple.

Pam—When Steve comes home from work, I try to be ready with a calm and well-ordered home. I give him a few minutes to get settled, check the mail and organize his gym bag for the next day's early morning swim. Then he makes his way into the living area of our home. We tell each other about our day. Sometimes there will be a small glass of wine waiting for him, and a bowl of his favorite brand of nuts. After dinner, we may have a meeting or phone call or we may sit and talk about our ideas, feelings, hopes, and dreams. Other times, we may watch a movie or read. All of these are simple ways that help us connect together emotionally.

Emotional oneness is, in a sense, a "dance." The longer Steve and I are together, the more deeply we feel connected in that dance. Whenever necessary, one of us lets the other know that the dance is not working as well as we'd like. So we make changes to make the dance smoother and more satisfying.

Steve and I feel that, for the most part, we have settled into a dance where we are growing emotionally closer as time goes by. We live together connecting soul-to-soul. We're walking in the same direction. There is harmony. This sizzle is what we believe God wants for every marriage.

But, you may say, what do I do if my spouse won't lift a finger and I am left to do everything? Resentment builds up when one spouse feels they are carrying more than their fair share. Prayer is the first plan of attack and then followed by gentle conversations. These must not be accusatory and must be spoken in kindness. For example, you might say, "When you leave the table and sit in front of the TV while I clean up everything, it makes me feel like you don't care about me. Can we clean things up together quickly, and then we can both relax together. That is very romantic to me." (Ladies, that last line is important. Don't miss it. Most men are not complicated.)

Spiritual and emotional oneness set the stage for passionate and meaningful physical oneness. As we said earlier, spiritual and emotional oneness are foreplay to the main event. It's best not to separate these because God created sex to be a glorious overflow of the soul connection between a husband and wife. Now we turn our attention to physical oneness and the chapter on sex that you have been waiting for.

Chapter Eight

Secret # 8

Have Sex Often

Steve—Sexual intercourse is an incredible celebration of the love between a husband and wife. And it's a vital part of a healthy marriage. In fact, one marriage expert we know suggests that a couple's sexual relationship is often a key indicator of the overall health of their marriage. Generally speaking, the more fulfilling sex life a married couple experiences, the healthier the marriage. This is one reason why Pam and I believe that having sex often is another secret to a sizzling marriage.

We are now both in our 60's, and Pam and I make love more often and even more passionately than the first few decades of our marriage. As a result of doing everything we've said in the previous chapters, our sex life is richer and fuller than ever. This is true not only during the normal routines of life at home but even more so when we are away on our "escapes" a few times a year. We believe this is what God intends for marriage.

Now, we hope you don't feel that we're being salacious when Pam and I speak about sexual intercourse in marriage. The truth is, if we left sex out of the conversation this would be a very incomplete book on marriage. God designed sex to be an essential part of marriage between a husband and wife. Everything we've said up this point sets the foundation for sizzling sexual intimacy in marriage.

Most of us realize that it is possible to experience the sex act, as just that—a physical act and not much more. Tragically, this is the essence of sex for some people. It is biology and not much else.

But God designed sex for more than merely physical pleasure and procreation. This is why God created sex to occur only with those who are married. Only within the covenant bond of marriage between a husband and wife can there be the kind of trust, friendship, tenacity-to-work-through-difficulties, commitment and the Holy Spirit's touch that unleashes sexual intercourse to become one of the most profound ways people can experience love.

Sex is a celebration of marriage love. If we look at it as a celebration of the love between a husband and wife, then sexual intercourse very much is something married couples should look forward to. However, it is also an area where many couples struggle. In the movie, "Hope Springs," husband (Tommy Lee Jones) and wife (Meryl Streep) had been married for a long time...but for many years they had slept in different bedrooms. As they meet with a therapist, the husband says that after he had been put off by his wife over and over again, he just turned "it" off. That is a revealing statement.

Pam and I have seen times when a husband has been sexually deprived, put off or ridiculed for so long that he eventually submerges his sexual desire and either turns "it" off (like in the movie) or turns to pornography or other inappropriate behaviors. We have also seen wives who have been so beaten down or devalued that sex becomes a dreaded chore rather than a delight.

Some marriages fall into a mode where the husband and wife are essentially roommates. All the to-dos get done, the bills get paid, and everything looks fine from the outside, but there is little or no sexual sizzle. This falls woefully short of God's robust intention for romance in marriage!

In my experience, marriages can begin to creep in the direction of becoming "roommates" when the husband's romantic initiatives toward his wife are met too frequently with rejection, humiliation, judgment or criticism. Or conversely, when the wife is not treasured and loved with a selfless and sacrificial love.

Thus, on the one hand, it is vital for a wife to understand that when she rejects her husband sexually, he can perceive her rejection as wholesale rejection of himself as a man. I have often told wives that they exert tremendous power over their husbands. What a wife does in the bedroom in a very real way can make or break her husband.

On the other hand, it is also vital for husbands to know that great sex begins at breakfast by honoring his wife, treating her kindly and serving her. As we said in the previous chapter, sizzling sex is an overflow from spiritual and emotional oneness. Gentlemen, you may have to trust me on this until you've experienced it. But the best sex is infinitely more than biology.

After decades of marriage and counseling with scores of married couples who are frustrated with the level of sexual intimacy they experience (which always falls short of the passionate love they see in movies or read about in books), Pam and I have come to realize how critical it is for the church to teach on this subject. If the church does not teach about God's wonderful gift of sex, then the only message people will hear is the distorted image portrayed in the media, books, and magazines.

As a result, Pam and I have taught about sex within marriage in our weekend services, and Pam teaches a seminar on sexual intimacy to our women every year. This seminar has had a profound impact on the lives of hundreds of women.

My wife and I have found Kevin Leman's book, *Sheet Music*, to be delightful. It is an excellent resource to get married couples talking together about their sexual relationship. We have recommended this book to scores of couples, and we almost always suggest that they read it out loud together. Far too many couples never discuss this important area of their marriage. Reading *Sheet Music* out loud together gives a married couple a vocabulary they can use to discuss their own sexual relationship.

One woman told Pam that her husband would never read any book with her. Pam suggested to her that she take off all her clothes, sit in bed and ask him to read one chapter of *Sheet Music* with her. Under those circumstances, we guarantee that most husbands will eagerly read the book!

Pam and I have a burden for the marriages around us. We mentioned earlier that one of the most frequent prayer requests at our church is for hurting marriages. I believe the devil is attacking marriages like never before. There are troubles and dangers everywhere we look. Life seems uncertain to many people. Because of this, we need vibrant marriages to be multiplied if we are to thrive in our chaotic world.

A sizzling Christian marriage is not only an example to the world of God's plan for a relationship with him, but it is also an example to our children and grandchildren. It is in the marriage relationship that we find the support and strength to carry on as a family. Yet marriages are in crisis everywhere, and this is why we are being so vulnerable sharing with you about our marriage.

Our church is one of many like-minded churches that share the Gospel and help people to learn to walk with Jesus as Lord. But if we don't teach about a God-centered marriage, how will our people know? How can we prepare people to thrive in these tumultuous times if we don't teach them the basics about marriage? Many couples accept Christ as their Savior, but they seem to live in the same way they did before crossing the line of faith. This is why we believe there has to be even more teaching about how to experience a vibrant Christian marriage.

With this in mind, we have some practical suggestions to share that we have learned over the years. We want you to imagine that you are sitting down across the table from Pam and me at a coffee shop. In the course of conversation, you ask us about marriage and sex. These are the things we would share with you as beloved friends and co-followers of Christ.

Pam's Sex Advice (Mostly for Wives)
Surrender Your Sexual Relationship to God

Pam—Wives, ask God to bless your intimacy and to give you the desire to please your husband in bed. Remember that God is the sex expert. Ask the Lord to heal your past, your fears, and your hurts. God desires that we live free from the lies we may have believed about ourselves, our bodies, our marriage, and lies about sex.

Pray for sweet and meaningful sexual encounters for the two of you together. If you are not crazy about sex because of past memories and fears, then I urge you to surrender those things to the Lord. God knows how important sex is to marriage and to your husband. Ask God for help in this area and trust that he will give you what you need. Get counseling if you need it.

Wives, if our first ministry is to our husband, then we are to meet his sexual needs. By fulfilling those needs, we are affirming his manhood as nothing else. In the book, *For Women Only*, author Shaunti Feldhahn interviewed over 1,000 men in all walks of life. What did these men want their wives to know?

> "Men want women to know that they want more sex than they are getting. They believe that the women who love them don't seem to realize that this is a crisis, not only for the man but for the relationship."

Sex fills a powerful emotional need in your husband. He needs to know that you find him desirable. His eyes will be less prone to wander if you tell him regularly that he is sexy and that you desire him.

Sex Makes Your Husband Feel Loved

If your husband is cranky, chances are he probably needs sex. If you wonder if this is true...try it and you'll see how sex amazingly transforms your husband's disposition.

But as women, we also feel out of sorts at times, and we can't put a finger on why. In my experience, if we let our husbands hold us close and make love to us, many times we end up feeling better about the world around us. So sex may also be the solution to making us feel better about ourselves, just like it does for our husbands. When a woman has an orgasm, it gives her an emotional and hormonal release that makes her feel loved. So, wives, let's get busy!

After a talk I gave about marital intimacy, a wife approached me with a true story about a wedding reception where her husband was employed as the DJ. After the bride and groom had their dance together, the parents and grandparents were invited to join them on the dance floor to give the bride and groom one piece of advice about a happy marriage.

One set of grandparents had flown all the way from England for the wedding. As the microphone was handed over to the very proper British grandmother, she said matter of factly in her adorable English accent, "Keep his stomach full and his balls empty!"

Evidently, the dance was postponed for quite some time while the DJ, the bride and groom and all the guests regained their composure. I love that story because, even though some may see it as a bit crass, there is considerable truth in it. Most men are not complicated. Sex helps a husband to feel that his wife loves him and believes in him like nothing else.

There are many marriages where the husband and wife cohabit under one roof, but not much more. This is definitely not God's plan for marriage. One reason this happens is too-frequent sexual rejection. Many men view taking a romantic initiative as a huge risk of being humiliated or feeling inadequate. They feel judged and criticized. When a wife rejects her husband's attempts to have sex, he can feel rejected as a man.

On the contrary, many husbands love to have their wives take the initiative by hinting around, planning getaways, romantic dinners, and other similar things. Doing those things lets a husband know that his wife is interested in having an intimate end of the evening.

Entice Each Other

Wives, make yourself someone that your husband will want to pursue. Take care of yourself. Don't be harried and tuned out to what is going on in his life. Make your husband your top priority as you seek to entice him. Be a student of your spouse. Be interesting. There have been times when Steve tells me that I am on my phone too much. So I put my phone away and give him my full attention. Simple things like this make a difference. Each time you do this, you will sow seeds for more passionate sexual encounters. Find what says "romance" to your man. Ask him. You may be surprised.

Steve thought that buying me flowers was a waste of

money since "they just die." But when I told him that buying me flowers was a very romantic gesture, it changed his point of view. He wants to romance me in my language so that I will want to romance him in his language—I'm sure you know what I mean!

Have a Healthy Self-Image

Wives, God has made you perfectly for your husband. Sometimes we think we want bigger breasts or to be 20 pounds thinner, or whatever else we think would make us "perfect." But in case you didn't know this, there is no perfect body. Your husband loves you for you. So let him enjoy your body!

However, I do want to remind you that sexual intercourse takes energy. Because of this, if a wife is not in decent physical condition to have passionate sex, then she needs to get to the gym and take better care of herself so she can celebrate her love with her husband! Enough said.

1 Corinthians 7:3-5 is a crucial passage about sex.
"The husband should fulfill his wife's sexual needs, and the wife should fulfill her husband's needs. The wife gives authority over her body to her husband, and the husband gives authority over his body to his wife. Do not deprive each other of sexual relations, unless you both agree to refrain from sexual intimacy for a limited time so you can give yourselves more completely to

prayer. Afterward, you should come together again so that Satan won't be able to tempt you because of your lack of self-control."

We see from this passage that a lack of sex in marriage may cause our spouse to have wandering eyes. But, wives, we dare not look at sex as merely a "duty" to fill our husband's needs. As you pray and ask God to give you freedom in this area of your life, hopefully, you will discover the joy of coming together with your husband to truly celebrate your love together.

Studies have shown that committed Christian marriages have more sex and enjoy it more than singles or couples who are not married. This is because God designed sex to be shared only within the bonds of marriage. God's way is always best. And God wants us to enjoy his gift of sex within marriage!

Get Enough Rest

Our society is running at top speed, and we often fall into bed exhausted with nothing left to give to our husband. When this happens, there is no time or energy to celebrate the sexual love God has given married couples. So, go to bed at a decent hour. Turn off the TV and don't stay up late. Take a short nap if you can.

I know countless mothers of young children who give of themselves all day to their children, and the thought of giving themselves to their husbands later that evening is downright offensive. They have nothing left. This is why it's so important to get enough rest. Adequate rest is a spiritual discipline. Wives, God does not want us to be so busy or exhausted that we don't have time and energy for sex with our husband.

Plan Time for Sex

Look at your week's calendar and make sure there is time for the two of you. Sex takes time. Someone said years ago that men are like microwaves and women are like crockpots. Don't rush sex. You need extended time to sexually celebrate your love.

Author Kevin Leman says in *Sheet Music*,
"Has your husband ever come up behind you, cupping a breast as you put mascara on your eyes only to have his hand slapped away with a curt 'Not now!'

"There's such a huge difference between a wife who slaps a man's hands away, and one who giggles mischievously, even engaging in one or two minutes of light petting, only to whisper in his ear, 'This sounds so delicious, but unfortunately I really do have to get ready for work. Let's save it for tonight when you'll get all you want and more.'

"The second woman will have fulfilled her husband, even while staying clothed and keeping her hair in place. The first wife will have deflated her husband and eroded his masculinity, all for the sake of sixty to ninety seconds. That's a costly minute!"

This illustration is convicting for all of us wives. If we can be more aware of our husband's attempts to reach out for us and receive them with love and a playful response, we will build him up and put a spring in his step without even taking off our clothes.

Arrange to have the children taken care of so you can go out on a date. Better yet, trade with another couple to keep your kids overnight, so you have all night alone. This takes intentionality. What happens more than we'd like to admit is that sometimes we go through life doing what needs to be done, but we don't ever think about surprising our husband or hinting around playfully about "looking forward to having you come home to me..." It doesn't take much. A short text to your husband that you have something "special planned" for him later that evening will fill him with joy and anticipation.

To boost your husband's confidence, tell him what a wonderful lover he is, or how you love his muscles and his body, or how attracted you are to him, or how he satisfies you. Never criticize him or make fun of his sexual performance.

That is lethal to a man. As wives, we have enormous power over our husband to help make him into a great man, but we can also emotionally cut him off at the knees. So, breathe life into your husband!

Teach Your Husband What Pleasures You

Many books I have read about sex suggest that wives have to teach their husbands what pleasures them. My personal experience also bears this out. Your husband wants to sexually arouse you, but you have to show him, you have to communicate with him, you have to coach him. Let him know when he does something that feels good to you.

On the other hand, you also need to ask him what he likes and how you can pleasure him. I am amazed at how many couples never talk about sex. You need to communicate. If this is something you have not developed in your marriage, then start the conversation slowly. We mentioned previously that *Sheet Music* is a great way to give you opportunities to talk about sex as you read the book together.

God Wants Wives to Feel Sexual Pleasure

Did you know that the clitoris has no function other than for a woman to feel sexual pleasure? Isn't that amazing?!

God created a special body part specifically so the woman would have pleasure in the marriage bed. Wives, if this is important to God, then it needs to be important to us as well!

Sometimes I am asked about "rules" in Scripture about sex. The Bible doesn't provide many "rules" about what we can and can't do in bed, but it does make it clear that sex is important in marriage. As a result, I believe that whatever is mutually agreed upon and enjoyed by both husband and wife is fine as you celebrate your love.

Wives, if you have trouble experiencing orgasms, try using a vibrator together with your husband. You may also need some bio-identical hormonal cream for vaginal health as you get older. Now, when I have mentioned about vibrators in my talks with wives, I have had a couple of comments about "sex toys" that are degrading. That is not at all what I am talking about. However, I don't believe there is anything wrong with helping the wife reach climax if this is a reoccurring problem.

Many medical professionals have women regularly ask for help with pain or dryness with intercourse. Be bold and read up on things you can do and don't be afraid to talk to your doctor. I urge you to consider sex as an extremely vital part of your marriage. If you need help, please get help.

Read Christian Books on Marriage and Sex

Doing it "in the buff" is even better! There are many helpful Christian books on marriage and sex. Put money in your budget to enhance your sex life. This may be things such as buying books to read together, new sheets, nights away together, lingerie, fun bed-time snacks, and other things like that.

Your marriage is worth investing in, and sex is an important part of marriage. Surprise your husband in a sexually arousing way. Take a bubble bath together. Give each other a massage using scented massage oils. Each time you make love can be a different experience. Get out of a rut and try some new things. Be adventuresome. Your husband will love you for it!

Make Your Bedroom a Special Place

I believe the master bedroom should be the most beautiful room in the house. This is where you celebrate your love together. Put a lock on the door if you have children or anyone else living in your house with you. Keep your bedroom neat and tidy. Don't leave the ironing board up or a heap of clean laundry to fold on your bed.

Make your bedroom a special place with candles, music and other ambiance enhancers. Get rid of old, torn, frumpy night clothes. Think of what you wore to bed when you first got married and compare it to what you wear to bed now.

Your husband needs to know that you are thinking of him when you chose what to wear to bed. Obviously, if you have children in the house, you will want to wear something modest, but it can still be pretty! Behind the locked door, though, make sure you wear something sexy (or nothing at all) so that your husband will be eager to join you in bed.

Let Your Husband Enjoy Your Body

It is important to note that many women are self-conscious about their bodies. A husband can say she is beautiful a million times, but that one comment, spoken in the heat of anger, or sarcastically mentioned in joking, will sear itself into a wife's soul and never be forgotten.

A husband has several challenges in marriage, but one that will probably take a lifetime of effort and prayer is to convince his wife that he loves her body—every part of her body. If a wife has a positive attitude about her body and knows that her husband is enthralled with it, she can relax and not be so self-conscious.

This has taken me years and years to understand. We

226

are shown on TV, in movies, and in magazines what we are "supposed" to look like. And we forget that those pictures have been air-brushed and altered to perfection. So a wife comes into her bedroom and undresses with one hand, and reaches for her robe with the other to cover herself before her husband can get a look at her "too thick mid-section" or "too small breasts," or whatever else she feels is not what it should be.

I think most wives would be surprised if they spent more time in the bedroom naked, putting on their makeup in the bathroom, sitting and talking to their husband, that they may see their husband is captivated with looking at her body.

But I have to say that husbands are the key to making their wife feel comfortable naked. A husband can't tell his wife often enough that she is beautiful. He has to tell her every day and throughout the day. And this means even more when it isn't covert initiation for sex.

One wife shared with me that throughout her pregnancies her husband told her that he didn't like how she looked. She was too fat. Another wife sadly confessed that her husband told her that she didn't look the same as when they got married...18 years earlier! What's wrong with these men?!

If a husband could only realize that what he says to

his wife about her body impacts significantly on how comfortable she is with sex. If a husband wants his wife to be more relaxed and free in bed, he has to convince her that her body is ravishing to him and that he wouldn't change a single thing.

Sex Begins in the Mind

Imagine the scene: The husband comes home from work and is looking forward to having a delightful time in bed with his wife that evening. The wife has also arrived home from a day at work, thrown dinner together while quizzing her daughter with her spelling words for the test tomorrow. The multi-tasking continues for the wife until she is finally able to lie down on her pillow. Not once has she even thought about sex or what the end of her evening would look like other than a yearning for her all-too-comfortable bed and deep, uninterrupted sleep.

The husband is surprised that the wife does not pick up on his "clues." The wife is hoping he doesn't know she is purposefully ignoring those "clues." So, what has gone awry? That morning, or sometime during the day, there could be a "checking in" to see how the other is doing... "having a nice day?" or "looking forward to tonight" kind of communication. Thinking about sex is one way to prepare for sex.

After receiving a sensuous text from her husband, the wife could respond with another sensuous text to let him know that she loves him. Then, as she continues through her afternoon, she can pray, and think about how she could make their evening special—get the kids to bed on time; not get involved in a movie, playfully greet her husband when he gets home, etc. Romance just doesn't "happen" when there are a million details to attend to throughout the day. You have to plan, prepare, and invest in your lovemaking because sex begins first in the mind.

Get Children Out of Your Bed

This is a problem for many couples—children often come first before the marriage. Remember that a strong marriage is one of the greatest gifts you can give your children. When there is a nightmare or illness, the children may need to come into mommy and daddy's bed briefly, but then they need to learn that they have their own bedroom. Work on it. It will be a gift that you give to your husband to not have children in your bed.

I have found an even more sensitive issue in the marriage bed are pets. One woman told me that her husband accused her of loving their dog more than him because she insisted on having the dog in their bed. If your pet is in any way getting in the way of your lovemaking, the pet should be in its own bed...period!

Pray Naked As a Couple

I have already mentioned it, but it is worth repeating. Praying is one of the most intimate things a married couple can do. When you are naked together, the prayer becomes about you as a couple, baring your soul to reach out to Almighty God who made you and desires the best for you as he loves you with his great and unending love.

I believe it puts a smile on God's face when a married couple prays naked together. It draws the couple together in oneness with Christ as the center. It ensures the wife that her husband is reaching for God's guidance in his attempts to be a better husband. And the husband also hears his wife seeking God to become the best wife possible for him. So, pray naked!

Steve's Sex Advice (Mostly for Husbands)
Sex Begins in the Morning

Steve—Husbands, you need to be aware that sex begins first thing in the morning. If you are even remotely thinking about romance later that evening, then you'd better be kind and gentle in the morning. I'll admit that women are still a bit of a mystery to me, but this much I have figured out—your wife does not become sexually aroused in the same way that you do.

Women tend to be more holistic than men. They do not compartmentalize as most men do. This means if you sow seeds of kindness and gentleness in the morning, you may reap some dividends later in the evening. But if you sow seeds of anger, sarcasm, hurt or apathy in the morning, generally speaking, you are probably in for a long, cold night ahead.

This is another way of saying everything we've already said up to this point in the book. When a husband is genuinely seeking Christ, it is sexy for most women of God. Becoming best friends with your wife is important foreplay for rich and meaningful sex. Selflessly serving your wife will make her feel valued, loved and honored, so that sex with you becomes a joy. Chances are that she will want to pleasure you in bed even more because you have taken such great care of her outside of the bed. Forgiving frees you both from the past so that you can fully embrace each other physically in the moment.

Lingering conversations are like nitroglycerin for marriage sex. Men, there is nothing more romantic for your wife than for you to share something deeply emotional with her. And when you are intentional about investing in your marriage relationship, watch out! Add to those things cultivating emotional oneness and praying naked together as you experience spiritual oneness—well, all those secrets combined help to lead to sizzling sex in marriage!

Gentlemen, please hear my heart in this. God designed sex to be much more than biology. When a husband and wife draw closer to Jesus, they also end up drawing closer to each other. And that often leads to better, more frequent and more passionate sex. So remember that sex begins in the morning with your tone of voice, your kind words, and your servant's heart.

Slow Down

The old adage "enjoy the journey" is quintessentially true with sex. Climax may be the hoped-for destination, but getting there is more than half the fun. Pam and I have repeatedly said in this book that great sex takes time — so, slow down and take your time!

With that in mind, it is essential for husbands to understand that his wife's sexual fulfillment should always come before his. Sex offers one of the most tangible ways for a husband to serve his wife. And, I might add, it is also one of the most pleasurable ways we serve her.

Foreplay is not second tier sex — foreplay is sex. This is especially true when both husband and wife have a growing spiritual and emotional connection. To help you with this, you might count how many times you tell your spouse that you love them as you make love. If those words do not come easily and often as you celebrate your marriage love, you may be going way too fast. Try giving each other a full body massage using baby oil. Better yet, do it in front of a fireplace.

Consider verbally loving each other as you make love physically. Tell your spouse how much you enjoy them physically. Admire each other's body. Whisper how blessed you are by the admirable characteristics you see in your spouse's life. Speak life into your spouse's soul even as you pleasure their body. Slow down!

A Wife's Orgasm Communicates Volumes

Back to *Sheet Music*, Kevin Leman comments that many husbands get more satisfaction from bringing their wives to orgasm than climaxing themselves. Wives, that is worth noting! Believe it or not, men are not always completely selfish when it comes to sex. Yes, some men are, but not all. Especially men who are growing in their walk with Christ. As the life of Christ grows in each of us, it causes us to become more and more selfless...even in the bedroom.

Pam and I want wives to know that their sexual responsiveness to their husband can be one of the greatest confidence boosters their man will ever have. Every orgasm a wife has communicates loudly to her husband that he "has what it takes."

What Happens in Bed
Must Be Mutually Agreed Upon

Whatever a husband and wife do in the bedroom must be mutually agreed upon. Sexual intercourse is a glorious celebration of marriage love. It is not fantasyland! The Bible teaches that *"Love is patient, love is kind...It does not dishonor others, it is not self-seeking"* (1 Corinthians 13:4-5).

Applying this to sexual activity in bed means if the husband wants to do something, but the wife does not—then it doesn't happen. And vice-versa. If the wife wants to do something but the husband does not—then it doesn't happen either. Love does not demand or manipulate. Love is not self-seeking. Love defers. Love puts the feelings of our spouse ahead of our own.

Romance Matters

I am a simpleton when it comes to food. In fact, my all-time favorite meal is a fried egg sandwich with a vanilla milkshake. Food is not an event for me. I eat to live, but I don't live to eat. As a result, spending money on a fancy meal at a nice restaurant seems to me to be wasteful. Why not stay home and I'll have a fried egg sandwich.

But Pam is wired very differently than me. A nice meal at an elegant restaurant is romantic to her—and romance matters. So, guess what? Every so often I take Pam out to a nice dinner. It puts a smile on her face, and that usually leads to bedtime activity for us at the end of the evening.

The point is this—to keep sizzle in your sex life, learn what says "I love you" for your spouse and do it as often as you can. Romance really does make a difference!

Pray While Making Love

Praying while making love can be a powerful experience. Husbands, I encourage you to pray for your wife as you physically love her. Wives, I encourage you to do the same as you physically love your husband. God is the author of sex. He delights when husbands and wives celebrate their love with sexual intercourse. Sex is not dirty or shameful. When a husband and wife share their love for each other with sexual intercourse, it is like shouting "Hallelujah!" to our loving Heavenly Father who created sex.

Be Creative

Wives, as you and your husband get older, he may need you to initiate more often. (In fact, he may need you to initiate all the time!) Erections that come at the drop of a hat when a man is in his 20's or 30's don't happen quite so readily in his later years. That does not mean that your husband is less interested in sex or that he wants it any less. But it may mean he needs a bit of gentle encouragement from you. Talk about this as a couple. Be open. If your husband seems to have "lost interest" it may mean that he's embarrassed about having less horsepower. But many times wives can help. Sex is a gift to be celebrated together by husband and wife. So, celebrate!

And be creative when health issues arise. We know some married couples that have had health issues which prevented them from having intercourse. They did not stop having sex...but they did have to become creative. They made lemon-aid out of lemons! In Pam's talk to wives about sexual intimacy, she mentions that if a wife has difficulty reaching orgasm, she might consider using a vibrator when making love with her husband. Get medical help if you need to. But, above all, be creative!

If a husband is totally unable to have an erection (because of medical issues), it does not necessarily mean the married couple must cease sexual activity. After all, the wife may still have a desire for sexual fulfillment. In that case, the husband can be creative and sexually stimulate his wife manually or orally to help her achieve orgasm. This is consummate selflessness, but isn't that what sex is all about?

Final Thoughts

Sex is a celebration of marriage love. Sex is helping your spouse to feel God's love for them through the lens of the pleasure you bring them in sexual intercourse. Sex is one of the greatest gifts that God has given married couples. Sex mirrors how much God loves us because marriage mirrors Christ's love for the church.

Gentlemen, the next time you make love to your wife, I encourage you to make love to her with God's love. Take your time. Shower her with your love. Enjoy every moment. Linger. Allow the pleasure that you both feel to be a reflection of God's intense and passionate love for you. And do it often!

Sex is clearly part of what Genesis means when Adam and Eve become one flesh. They experienced sexual intercourse as husband and wife—and I'm sure they enjoyed it! But I hope you can see how spiritual oneness and emotional oneness feed the joy and intimacy of sexual intercourse—each one builds on the other. When a married couple keeps growing in spiritual oneness and keeps growing in emotional oneness, then their physical oneness moves to a sizzling new level.

This is also why pornography and casual sex come up empty. They might seem thrilling for a while. However, in the end, pornography and casual sex always lose their luster because sex is designed to be much more than merely a physically stimulating activity. The fact is, God designed sex to be the overflow of our soul-love in marriage. So when a husband and wife are drawing closer and closer in their spiritual oneness and closer and closer in their emotional oneness, it amplifies their physical oneness. And this leads to sexual sizzle in marriage that never gets old!

A Husband's Prayer
For His Sexual Relationship with His Wife

Dear Lord,

Thank you for the amazing gift you have given me with my wife. Help me to treasure her as we make love together. Help me to remind her of her beauty. Help me to speak words of life to her as we make love together.

Thank you for the wonderful way you have designed our bodies to fit perfectly. As I make love to my wife, help me to communicate to her soul the lavish way that you love her. Help my wife to feel the cascading waterfalls of your love through me.

I pray that you would help me to pleasure my wife in a powerful way. Help me...
* *to touch her with your touch,*
* *to kiss her with your kiss,*
* *to love her with your love.*

Lord, thank you for the glorious gift of sex between a husband and wife! We invite you to smile upon us as we sexually celebrate our love for each other!

In Jesus' Name!

Amen

Chapter Nine

Secret #9

Release Disappointments

Steve—We were in the Chilean town of Villa Alemana in March 1985. Pam was pregnant with Tommy. In that era, most churches in Chile held their services on Sunday evenings. We would often travel to a different church every week where I would be a guest speaker. Normally we would leave our three girls at home with a babysitter since the services got out quite late. But that particular Sunday our babysitter couldn't make it, so we took all three with us.

Many Sundays we would arrive before the service for "once," which is an early evening tea with sandwiches. This particular Sunday we had all enjoyed time around the table with the pastor and his family. Our girls sat politely and drank tea that had cooled in their saucers and ate the small finger sandwiches and cookies. After "once" I took Rachel and Jennifer out to the dirt road in front of the house while Pam visited with the ladies in the kitchen with our four-year-old Christina.

Suddenly the ground started shaking violently, and it sounded like a freight train was passing right through the middle of the wooden two-story house. Pam is from Southern California, and she had been in earthquakes previously. So she knew what to do—stand in the doorway; it is supposed to be stronger. But after the buffet and refrigerator toppled over, she decided that she didn't want to remain anywhere inside because the entire house was swaying from side to side like a drunken sailor. So, she picked up Christina, and they stumbled out the front door.

The ground was moving so herky-jerky that people had to hang onto trees so they wouldn't fall over. Pam slowly swayed her way toward me. I was sitting with Rachel and Jennifer on the curb in the street. Pam and Christina finally made it to us, and we all watched incredulously as our VW van bounced up and down off the dirt road. People were running, screaming and yelling. It was like a horror movie!

Then a funny thing happened. A little lady from the church—in her late 60's and not more than five feet tall—calmly walked into the street and began preaching to the neighbors who were running around and screaming. She shouted at the top of her lungs: "Are you ready to meet your God? Do you know Jesus as your Savior? Are you ready?"

It was an amazing sight! The quake lasted three very long minutes and registered 8.0 in intensity, leaving more than a million people in Chile homeless.

The earthquake proved to be a life-altering event for a vast number of people. Many of our neighbors were so fearful about weathering the aftershocks in their poorly built homes that they slept in their cars for days.

Pam and I were still young. But that earthquake was the first of many unexpected and very difficult intrusions in our life. (We were without water for 13 days). I'm not certain if it was poor theology or naïveté. But for many years those speed bumps caught Pam and me off-guard. We somehow expected things to be easier. We loved Jesus and were faithfully serving him. I think in the back of our mind we believed that the Lord would protect our family from painful valleys. But we live in a broken world and life throws us curve balls. Things happen. Relationships get sour. Jobs end. Accidents take place. People (including us) make poor choices—and the list of life's disappointments mount up. These scenarios can have a dramatic impact on marriage! As a result, Pam and I have discovered another vital secret to a sizzling marriage is to release disappointments.

When we were first married, I remember seeing two older couples in a restaurant. One couple stared blankly off into the distance. There was no conversation or warmth between them. It was obvious they had been together for a long time. But if there ever was any sizzle in the relationship, it appeared to have completely ended.

In contrast, another older couple a few booths away was eagerly engaged in conversation; they held hands, and their relationship oozed with warmth and joy. Since I didn't speak to either couple, I will never know for certain. But I wonder if the lifeless couple had let the disappointments drain the sizzle out of their relationship, while perhaps the spunky couple had learned the secret of releasing them.

Pam—Everyone experiences disappointments. Perhaps it's disappointment from someone's hurtful words or actions. Maybe it's a forced retirement, health issues, financial setbacks, the loss of a loved one, the loss of a dream, decisions that our children have made, or even disappointment with ourselves. Disappointments are woven into the fabric of everyone's life.

And they are painful! So much so that we have known married couples that have been unable to release their disappointments and, as a result, they basically shut down emotionally. The spark has vanished from each of their eyes and numbness took its place. There was no more warmth, sizzle, joy, hope, or love. When we emotionally shut down like that, it closes the door for love to flow out or for love to flow in.

As a result, disappointment can contribute to serious trouble in marriage. For example, the percentage of divorces that occur after the loss of a child is extremely high. When disappointment is allowed to fester by rehearsing it over and over, it grows into bitterness and resentment. This affects all of our relationships, including marriage. We end up looking at life through the lens of our disappointment, and it colors everything. Over time, this can suck the life out of a marriage.

Surrender to God

The longer I walk with Christ, the more I realize the importance of surrendering to him completely. I believe this is the most crucial key to getting beyond our disappointments. The truth is God never asks us to carry our burdens alone. On the contrary, he tells us to cast our burdens on him. *"Cast all your anxiety on him because he cares for you"* (1 Peter 5:7).

I remember seeing a picture in my mind of me rolling a massive boulder up a steep hill. I was panting and struggling to move it forward. Jesus was standing next to me saying, "Wow! That is a heavy load! You are really working hard at this. Hmmm. You know, I could help you, if you let me." It took a bit, but then I stepped aside and let Jesus take over. He picked it up with one finger and flicked it away as you would flick a fly off your arm. I realized that I was trying to carry too many things myself instead of surrendering them to the Lord. Now I try to spend time each day surrendering to Jesus every situation, including every disappointment.

It helps not only to surrender the disappointing situation or person but also my feelings about the situation or person. Usually, our feelings don't change immediately after we make the choice to forgive and release. But making the choice is the first step and feelings may eventually follow. This is why surrendering my feelings has been helpful. To be sure, this is not a magic pill that works instantly, but it has been a meaningful step in the process of releasing my disappointments.

I am a consummate people pleaser, so my greatest disappointments have to do with people. I was raised hearing often from my parents "just don't disappoint us."

That instilled a fear in me to never disappoint others. But no one is perfect, including me. So occasionally I do disappoint people; not intentionally or premeditatedly, but most assuredly. This reality has given me a bit more grace when others disappoint me. But it is still hard! I have a hard time letting go. I struggle to release. This is one of the areas that God has been working on in my life for many years.

Steve—So why is surrender so hard for many of us? Worry is often the culprit. We relive situations, we weigh all the "what ifs," and we run the details over and over in our mind trying to find a way to "fix" the dilemma, the hurt that's been caused or the poor decision that has been made. We literally take the string of our thoughts and twist them and tie them into knots. Sadly, our emotions can be taken captive by this pattern and we walk around as if we're holding our breath...never really exhaling.

In the face of this, scripture tells us to lay our cares in God's hands, not to worry or fret, and to not be afraid, because our God is with us. And he is. His name is Emmanuel—God with us!

To help overcome worry, I have often pictured myself taking a handful of worry and laying it at the foot of the cross, then backing away with my hands behind my back so I can't pick it up. After doing this, every time I choose to worry I realize that I am picking the burden back up again. Jesus tells us, *"Come to me, all you who are weary and burdened, and I will give you rest. Take my yoke upon you and learn from me...For my yoke is easy and my burden is light"* (Matthew 11:28-30). This is an invitation to allow Jesus to carry our burdens. But this takes practice because surrender to the Lord is rarely once and done.

I have discovered that surrender begins in my heart by praising God for who he is and reminding myself of his greatness and power, his sovereignty and his loving-kindness. Then I exhale several times, and each time I exhale, I give my worry to the One who wants to carry my burdens. I imagine his presence with me at my side.

Throughout the day, every time my mind begins to lean toward worry, I take captive that thought and repeat the breathing exercise. Then I praise him for taking my worry and fear and replacing it with his peace.

Surrender is waving a white flag that says, "I can't but, Lord, you can. You are able, so I let go. I rest in the truth that nothing is impossible for you, O Lord." This helps me to anchor my thoughts and emotions in the Lord rather than allowing them to bounce around inside me like a pinball machine.

Practice means doing something over and over again. And sometimes I have to repeat this exercise over and over again until I receive the peace that he promises. And, just like practicing sports or a musical instrument, it gets easier over time.

Each time I surrender, it adds depth to my faith regarding who God is. Each time I surrender I find the peace that God promises: *"You will keep in perfect peace, those whose minds are steadfast, because they trust in you. Trust in the Lord forever, for the Lord, the Lord himself, is the Rock eternal"* (Isaiah 26:3-4).

Claim the Promises of Scripture

Pam—In addition to surrendering, claiming the promises in Scripture has been another helpful step for me to release disappointments. Since God is sovereign, he knows everything from the beginning to the end. And because he sees the whole picture, I can trust him with my disappointments, even when I can't understand. God promises to be with us and to give us the strength that we need. *"So do not fear, for I am with you; do not be dismayed, for I am your God. I will strengthen you and help you; I will uphold you with my righteous right hand"* (Isaiah 41:10).

God can carry us through the most painful disappointments and actually bring good out of them! This happens as these experiences spur my spiritual growth, strengthen my faith and give me more wisdom for the counseling I do with women.

Have Long-Term Vision

We mentioned this before, but it bears repeating...we are all broken. There is no such thing as a perfect person, a perfect marriage, or a perfect family. Every family has its "stuff." Ours is no different. What may be unique with us is that we have been in vocational ministry for four decades and our children grew up as MK's (missionary kids) and PK's (pastor's kids).

Some of our children felt the pressure of those expectations. I don't believe you can understand what that does to a child unless you have personally experienced it. Because of this, we will be circumspect in sharing details about what we have faced. We don't want to bring back "the fishbowl" and say anything that might disparage any of our children. However, we want to say enough to clarify that we have had some struggles. Learning to release these has been vital for our marriage not only to survive but also to continue to sizzle.

It has also helped to pray with long-term vision. When I was pregnant with each of our four children, both Steve and I prayed for our soon-to-be-born babies. We also prayed for them often as they grew up.

When they graduated from high school, I gave each one the stack of prayers I prayed for them from my prayer notebook. Just as I have done with praying for my husband, I recorded the answers in red. Those pages were a testimony of God's grace and goodness in their lives. I always felt that praying for our children was the greatest gift I could give them. And today I continue to pray for them and their families.

We were determined that our kids would not be among the statistics of children from ministry households who turn away from the Lord or his church. It was a huge part of my prayers! I firmly believed that if I prayed enough for my children, they would always follow God faithfully. However, as time has passed, I have learned that each of my children is on their own spiritual journey. This has resulted in me now having much more long-tern vision.

A few years ago, I was reading in Genesis about Jacob. I remember asking God why he chose Jacob to be the father of his chosen people. After all, as a young man, he was a liar, a cheat, and a manipulator. I thought, "Now, Mary, the mother of Jesus...good choice God! But Jacob? Really?"

Then, as I studied the life of Jacob, I realized that who he was as a young man was very different from who he was later in life. One of the last things scripture says about Jacob is that he *"worshiped as he leaned on the top of his staff"* (Genesis 47:31).

Now, how did he get from being a lying, cheating, manipulator to a man who worshiped God? Well, looking at his life, we see that he first went to live with his Uncle Laban, who was also a liar, a cheater, and a manipulator. So Jacob got a taste of his own medicine.

Then Jacob married two sisters. I imagine there was no peace in his home. The older sister had children right away, and the younger sister was married for many years before finally conceiving her two sons. There had to be plenty of snotty comments, complaining, dissension and rivalry between them. God knew just what Jacob needed to mold and shape his character.

This theme is woven throughout his life. Jacob had a parting of the ways with his brother Esau and lived in fear because he had stolen Esau's birthright. Jacob wrestled with the angel of God, and his hip was put out of joint. Jacob would not let go until God blessed him.

In truth, God was with Jacob on his entire journey. God knew what needed to be rooted out of Jacob's soul. God is sovereign, and when he called Jacob as a young man, even though he was a liar and a cheat, the Lord could see decades ahead who Jacob would become—a man who leaned on his staff and worshiped.

That lesson was a breakthrough for me concerning my adult children. From that point, I began praying with more long-term vision. Now, I am believing that God sees my adult children for who they are going to become. He knows their journey. He knows what they need to go through. He is sovereign. So, my prayers have changed to "Thy will be done, Lord, in my child's life."

This has allowed me to release my disappointments, which has greatly contributed to Steve and I enjoying an incredibly sweet season in our marriage. It hasn't always been this way. There have been times when I was only as happy as the least happy of my four children. My emotions went up and down like a roller coast. That was difficult for me personally and for our marriage. But now I rest more consistently in the truth that God is all-powerful and all-loving.

In addition, as I wait for God to answer my prayers, he is doing a work in me that is nothing short of miraculous. You see, years ago, when my kids were younger and under my roof, I was a very prideful mother. I loved telling others about how spiritual my kids were. Looking back, I'm sure I was a thorn in the flesh for those moms whose kids were doing disappointing things. I was not especially sensitive to the bleeding hearts that are often in hurting parents.

But God has used our own children's struggles to humble us where we very much needed to be humbled. I no longer brag about my kids. I love them dearly. But I no longer share their successes with prideful motivations.

So, what does this have to do with marriage? Tons! As Steve and I have weathered the ups and downs of our children, we have been through the gamut of emotions. There were times we were so numb we couldn't speak. We couldn't make love. We felt dead inside. We cried separately, and we cried together. We blamed ourselves, and we blamed each other. Sadly, at times, I even blamed God.

But God knew we needed to be knocked to our knees. And that is where we continue—on our knees praying for our adult children with long-term vision. On my "down days," Steve encourages me and reminds me of God's sovereignty and grace. He prays for me and with me. On his "down days" I try to do the same for him.

Steve—In my case, long-term vision meant viscerally coming to terms with Romans 8:28. Either it is true, or it is not. *"And we know that in all things God works for the good of those who love him, who are called according to his purpose."* Now, I am a firm believer in the inerrancy of Scripture. As a result, my head knows that Romans 8:28 is very much true. But my heart wrestled with this when it came to some of my greatest disappointments. However, a point came where I determined to trust God and his Word, even if I could not see evidence that anything was happening.

This was a liberating moment that allowed the pain of my disappointments to release their grip on me. I trust that God is at work in me and in those I love. Even when I can't see it, I now have a more long-term vision that can see beyond the disappointments to future days of redemption and spiritual renewal.

Cling To The Lord

Clinging to the Lord has also helped us to overcome disappointments. One of the unique issues that Pam and I face in ministry is when someone we love leaves our church. I believe this is true for every pastor. It doesn't matter if your church attendance is 50 or 5,000.

In our case, we planted Summit Christian Church. It is part of us. If you don't like our church, you must not like us. I know that sounds dramatic, but it is very hard not to take it personally when someone leaves Summit because they are not happy about whatever they are not happy about. This is my issue. I know it.

But, like every other kind of disappointment, the question is—what do we do with our hurt, so it doesn't turn into bitterness and resentment that creates a chasm in our soul and in our marriage? I hope it doesn't sound trite, but one way we release these things so we don't carry any "excess baggage" is to cling even more tightly to the Lord.

Focus on the Blessings Not the Losses

When we left our ministry in Wisconsin, there was a great deal of hurt and disappointment. After six years serving people we loved dearly, internal turmoil infected the congregation, and I eventually resigned as their Senior Pastor. Our family then moved out west to northern Nevada to plant a church. This was a terrible time to move our four teenagers. Our oldest had just graduated from high school, our second daughter was going into her senior year, our third daughter was a sophomore, and our son was going into 8th grade.

Was it easy? No. Our kids would sit on the front porch of our home, and as a car drove by, they would say (with their fingers in the shape of an "L"), "Hi, will you be my friend? I have no friends. I'm from Loserville, population one." This eventually became a joke in our family, and we now laugh about it. But at the time there was deep sadness, loss, and disappointment in all of us for the relationships we had left behind in Wisconsin.

Our first year held many blessings as we saw the hand of God start a new church family in the YMCA in Sparks, Nevada. It was tough for all of us, but our kids stepped up to the plate and sang on the worship team, manned the over-head projectors and welcomed those who entered the doors. Our four kids were the first faith heroes of our new church!

The following July, when we had completed one year in Nevada, God gave Pam an idea to make an altar of stones in our backyard. We did this as a family, and each of us wrote a verse or a prayer on a smooth river rock. This was a special time for the six of us. The kids also each wrote a letter to God which we still have in our files.

This story illustrates how we overcame the dis-appointment of leaving our friends and ministry in

Wisconsin. Instead of mourning endlessly all that we had lost, we recounted how God had met us in our disappointment. We thanked him for knowing what was best for us and we gave him the glory. In other words, we celebrated and praised God for what we did have; and we chose not to dwell on all that we had lost.

Pam and I did not know it at the time, but many more disappointments would come our way in the years ahead. Each of these could have sucked the life out of our marriage if we allowed it. But, instead, on our best days, Pam and I have chosen to praise God for what we do have and not bemoan who or what we may have lost.

Admittedly, we have walked this out in some seasons better than others. But I am convinced that one reason Pam and I enjoy the many blessings we share in our marriage is because, when we have faced disappointments, we have worked hard to focus on the blessings we still have and not be overly fixated on the losses.

Praise

Pam—Habakkuk 3:17-19 says,

"Though the fig tree does not bud and there are no grapes on the vines, though the olive crop fails and the fields produce no food, though there are no sheep

in the pen and no cattle in the stalls, yet I will rejoice in the Lord. I will be joyful in God my Savior. The Sovereign Lord is my strength; he makes my feet like the feet of a deer, he enables me to go on the heights."

Habakkuk's situation was the worst imaginable. But the tiny three letter word "yet" stands between the dire losses he saw all around him and his choice to praise God for the strength to go forward with hope and purpose. The Amplified Bible says, *"Yet [I will choose to] rejoice in the Lord; I will [choose to] shout in exultation to the [victorious] God of my salvation!"* (Habakkuk 3:18)

The choice to praise God in the midst of the storm is generally a choice we have to make over and over again. Usually, this isn't once and done. When life gets tough, and the disappointments mount up, we often need to choose praise over despair on a moment by moment basis.

The choice to praise God in the midst of difficulties is a choice only we can make, and it goes against our human nature. But it gets our focus off the problem and puts the spotlight on God, our Sovereign King. In Hebrews 13:15, the author exhorts the readers to *"continually offer to God a sacrifice of praise—the fruit of lips that confess his name."* This type of praise is similar to Habakkuk's. It is spoken out of anguish and determination.

Now, I am not a farmer, nor do I have vineyards. I do not have sheep and cattle in the stalls. But, similar to Habakkuk, I have experienced things that caused great fear and emotional pain. In those times, I have often rephrased his statement substituting my situation for the sheep, cows and produce. And then I declare to God in heaven that "Yet will I praise you!" When I set my heart on praise, my perspective changes.

You might say that the disappointment is so great that you don't have enough energy to praise. I get it. But let me tell you about a dear friend and fellow missionary who, years ago, was extremely ill in the hospital. I will never forget her telling me that even though she didn't have the energy to talk, she cupped her hands upward beside her on the bed in an attitude of praise. There have been times I have done the same when there were no words to express to God how I felt at that moment.

Praise has become something Steve and I enjoy doing together. Sometimes this is done when we pray naked in bed. More and more, when we pray together, praise comes because we have so much to praise and thank God for. God has used our praises to help us release our disappointments.

Don't Get Stuck In Grief

A final way we have learned to release our disappointments is by not getting stuck in our grief. Several years ago, I got a call from my sister that my mom had fallen and broken her hip. I immediately drove over to my parent's apartment, picked up my dad (who was using a walker) and then went to the hospital. That event started a journey for Steve and I that would result in major changes in our lives. While my mom went through surgery and rehab, I stayed with my dad a couple of nights, sleeping on the couch, and then brought him to our house to stay while my mom was recovering.

During those days in my parents' home, I noticed the drastically overdue expiration dates on many of the items in the refrigerator. Along with other observations, I came to the conclusion that my parents were not able to take care of themselves as we had thought. After talking to my three sisters and my parents, it was decided my parents would come to live with us full-time.

However, our house had stairs, so it was not conducive to my dad with a walker and my post-hip-surgery mom. To make a long story short, we put our house up for sale. It sold in a matter of days, and we moved, with my parents, into an apartment for seven months while a new house, with no steps, was built.

The first week in October, we moved into our new home with my parents, and for the next four months, my dad was in and out of the hospital. After his release in February, we finally decided to get hospice. Shortly after, on Valentine's Day, from his new bedroom, in the new house—the same house that had brought him such joy as he watched it being built—my father went to be with the Lord. And although I mourned his death deeply, I was not disappointed as we were expecting it for several years. What I chose to focus on instead was the joy and fun we had living together in our tiny apartment.

A week after his funeral services, we had a mission trip to Cambodia planned. We left the USA with the blessing of my mom who appeared to be in great health. However, upon arriving in Phnom Pen two days later, we were informed that my mom had suffered a heart attack. My sister was with her in the hospital, and we were told that she was doing well. So we decided to finish out our week in Cambodia.

Two days before we came home, my mom suffered a massive stroke. We were able to FaceTime with my sister, and she told us that my mom would not live much longer. My sister held the iPad next to my mom's face so I could see her and tell her good-bye. She was unresponsive, but we were believing that she could hear me.

Thirty minutes later, my phone rang with the news that mom had just passed. So, three weeks after my dad's funeral, we were back in the same worship center with family and friends. Numb? In shock? Disappointed? All of the above. I was looking forward to spending time with my mom when we got home. Should we not have gone to Cambodia?

Grief is a weird animal. But it is certainly another category of disappointment. Steve lost three of his four grandparents while we were on our first term in Chile. A few years later, he got a phone call (two weeks before our son was born) informing him that his dad had committed suicide. Grief can do a number on your marriage.

Shock, pain, numbness, regret, sadness. I sure didn't understand grief when Steve was going through it with his dad. I wish I had known then what I know now. I could have supported him much better. *The Grief Recovery Workbook* by John W. James and Russell Friedman was a great help to me after the loss of my parents.

Steve was also there for me. He let me be alone when I needed to be alone, loved me when I needed to feel his touch, and he let me take the time to work through the steps in *The Grief Recovery Workbook*.

My husband would look at me with a look on his face that said, "I don't understand, but I am here." Death is a disappointment that every marriage will face. I know someone who seems to have never worked through the losses in his life, and it has taken a toll on him emotionally and physically. We have also known marriages that have gotten stuck in their grief. Instead of moving closer to each other, the couple drifted away and shut down all emotions and love-making.

Steve—Disappointment, hurt, heartache. We can expect them because they are part of life. I could not count the number of times as I was leaving a hospital room or after hearing what someone is going through when I have said: "I can't imagine not knowing Christ at times like these! People who do not know Christ have no hope and nothing to hold on to. What a sad place to be."

The painful disappointments that Pam and I have experienced have equipped us to minister to the many hurting people that God brings our way. I shutter to think how prideful we would be if we had not gone through those circumstances. And I'm certain our marriage would not have any sizzle at all if we had not released those disappointments to God.

God is sovereign, and he knows precisely what each of us need to go through to learn to "lean on our staff and worship him," like Jacob. The Lord empowers us to keep moving forward in this life. Pam and I have chuckled when facing disappointments that at least God didn't tell us to marry a prostitute, like Hosea. And he didn't tell us to lie on our right side for six months, and then on our left side for six months like Ezekiel. Many things could be worse!

Jehoshaphat was on a mountain with Israel as their enemies gathered below. Jehoshaphat's prayer is one that Pam and I have said a number of times while laying in bed, staring up at the ceiling, *"Lord, we don't know what to do, but our eyes are fixed on you"* (2 Chronicles 20:12).

In those times of desperation, God has come close to us as a married couple. And we have found ways to release our disappointments so that our marriage continues to sizzle. We surrender our disappointments to God, we claim the promises in Scripture, we cling to God, we focus on the blessings instead of the losses, we offer a sacrifice of praise, and we have chosen not get stuck in our grief.

These have worked for us, and we hope they help you, too, because Pam and I want your marriage to sizzle. But for that to happen, both husband and wife must learn to release their disappointments.

Chapter Ten

Secret #10

Keep Dreaming Together

Pam—Every bride and groom begins their marriage with dreams. They dream about their wedding, they dream about their new home, they dream about what life will be in the future, and they dream about growing old together. However, as life unfolds, often the couple's shared dreams begin to wither.

This is tragic because Steve and I have discovered that dreams are vital for a robust marriage. In the same way that the frequency and passion of our sexual relationship can be a barometer of the health of our marriage, so too are the frequency and passion of our dreams. This is why Steve and I believe that a tenth secret for a sizzling marriage is to keep dreaming together.

After all these years, my husband and I still look forward to new adventures and new challenges. It tickles my bones that even in our 60's there is still so much more to experience!

I remember thinking when I was younger what it would be like to grow old with my husband. And that time is suddenly upon us. Now, thankfully, we usually don't feel old. But the reality is, now and then, our bodies let us know the reason that we both qualify for senior discounts.

These days my favorite passage in the Bible is 2 Corinthians 4:16-18.

> *"Therefore we do not lose heart, though outwardly we are wasting away, yet inwardly we are being renewed day by day. For our light and momentary troubles are achieving for us an eternal glory that far outweighs them all. So we fix our eyes not on what is seen, but on what is unseen. For what is seen is temporary, but what is unseen is eternal."*

It is awesome knowing that even though our bodies are getting older, the most important part of us—our soul—is being renewed day by day. This inspires me to invest effort and time cultivating my soul. The truth is if we spent as much time and money taking care of our soul as we do taking care of our physical body, we'd be in terrific spiritual shape and glow with the presence of Christ.

As the years go by, we also need to keep in mind the extraordinary dreams God has for us. *"No eye has seen, no ear has heard, no mind has conceived what God has prepared for those who love him"* (1 Corinthians 2:9). God has huge plans and purposes for us! And those are far greater than a fancy house and an exotic car. God has visions and dreams for us in both this life and the life to come. What we experience in this life is merely a shadow compared to what it will be like in heaven. Now that is exciting!

This has enormous implications for marriage because dreaming together helps to keep our marriage alive. Every once in a while Steve will ask me, "Where do you want to be and what do you want to do in three years? Or five years? Or ten years?" It's always a lively discussion! We learn about each other's dreams and what is important to each of us.

Right now, God willing, we think that we will remain at Summit for several more years. We dream of building a new worship center that will complete the campus we first opened many years ago. We don't know how long we are going to live, but we also dream about spending more time in Chile to help with leadership development in the churches we worked with 30-plus years ago. Once we've completed our current role at Summit, we've also dreamed about possibly serving a few months a year in an ex-patriot church in a Spanish speaking country. Steve dreams about writing more.

As for me, personally, I'd love to find a cabin in the woods within an hour's drive of us, where our children and grandchildren could visit. I also dream of using the cabin to bless ministry friends with getaways. I don't know if it will happen, but dreaming like this puts sizzle into our marriage.

Now, I have a hard time not getting on my "soap-box" about this, but sadly, many older married couples seem to have no greater dreams than to watch their favorite television show or to follow their favorite sports team. But what would it be like if couples our age, or older, asked God, "Lord, you know that I'm going to retire soon. What is it that you would have me do? I want a life of meaning and purpose. I don't want to coast until I die. I want to make a difference!"

Studies have uncovered a new phenomenon. Sociologists are calling it the "Third Adulthood." For the first time in history, people are retiring and living 20 to 30 more years. In previous eras, people retired and then, generally, died soon after. But people are living longer. And this third-adulthood population has experience, wisdom, resources and time. The potential kingdom impact is mind-boggling! But nothing will happen until a married couple begins to dream.

With that in mind, if you are facing retirement in the next few years, or are now retired, would you ask God if there is something greater he has for you? Would you be willing to serve with your spouse in a ministry where you both give of yourselves to bless others? Doing that together will help to put sizzle into your marriage. Serving together as a couple can be sexy. Try it!

Steve—Dreams also fuel younger married couples. In fact, if dreams die, the marriage may not survive. Dreams are to a marriage what oxygen is for the body—they are essential. When Pam and I were younger, we always had short-term dreams that kept us energized and forward-looking.

These dreams were simple—next summer's family vacation, a get-away with just the two of us, or reaching a financial milestone we had set. The key for us has always been agreeing together what the dream is, and then talking and praying about it together as we pursued it. Half the fun of our family vacations and our getaways as a couple has been the anticipation of looking forward to the experience. Such is the power of dreams!

As a couple, Pam and I have also had dreams about how God might use us. I mentioned earlier that I never wanted to live the "normal" suburban American dream. I had no interest in having 2.2 kids and 1.6 cars. Average was never my cup of tea. I wanted God to use us in a mighty way to make a huge difference for the cause of Christ. Because of this, Pam and I talk relentlessly about our ministry. It's never been "my ministry." It's always been "our ministry." So we dream together about what God could do next. Now, these dreams extend way beyond our ministry at Summit.

Dreams have fueled our marriage in an essential way. This is why we believe this tenth and final secret to a sizzling marriage is so vital—keep dreaming together!

How to Keep Dreams Alive
Spiritual Health

Pam—Healthy dreams flow from a healthy soul. Thus, the first step to keep your dreams alive is to nurture a healthy soul.

Each January I re-build my prayer notebook. A new page is added for that year for myself, for each member of my family, for my friends, and for our ministry. I also pray for two or three spiritual goals for that new year. These may include a desire to know God in a deeper way or an area of my life I want to have victory in.

These spiritual goals appear at the top of my "personal" page in my prayer notebook. As a result, I see them several times each week over the course of the year. As things happen to demonstrate how God is answering these prayers,

I note them down in red ink. Looking back over the year, I am always amazed how God works in my life, to mold me to become more like Jesus.

Steve has similar rhythms that keep him spiritually healthy—and this allows God to speak new dreams into us as we move forward in life. God is the ultimate dreamer! As we mentioned earlier, *"No eye has seen, no ear has heard, no mind has conceived what God has prepared for those who love him"* (1 Corinthians 2:9).

But Steve and I have discovered that in order for God to speak to us about his dreams, it is vital to be spiritually healthy. This avoids the blockages from sin or selfishness that might prevent us from hearing God's voice.

We mentioned at the beginning of the book the essential habits for spiritual health that we have practiced our entire married life. These habits include an active connection with a local church where we worship corporately, serve joyfully, give financially, connect with others and have spiritual accountability.

Spiritual health is reflected in our obedience to these basic Christian behaviors. This is important because dreams that are God-honoring are never self-serving, nor are they pursued in isolation from Christian community. Thus, the first step to keep dreams alive is to cultivate a healthy soul.

Time & Space

Steve—We also need time to consider our dreams. Dreamers don't generally live life at warp speed. This begs the question: How will your dreams as a couple flourish if every minute of your week is packed with endless activity? We can't have it all. Saying yes to dreaming will probably mean we have to say no to several other things.

To open up about dreams, Pam and I also need privacy. We need to be alone. We are empty nesters at the moment, so we can find time to be alone without too much effort. Other married couples may need to talk about dreams on a date night. Having the privacy to dream together allows both husband and wife to share at their own speed, and discuss the feelings that accompany their dreams. Unnecessary interruptions make it difficult to stay on track.

This is an obvious dividend of our periodic escapes as a couple. When Pam and I go away alone for several days, sheltered from the distractions and pressures of normal life, we find ourselves frequently discussing our dreams. Dreams are also a repeated topic when we drift into one of our lingering conversations.

Safety

P am—Obviously, if a relationship is not safe, there will probably not be much dreaming together. Sharing our dreams can be vulnerable. For me to share, I have to feel that my dreams will not be laughed at by Steve. Similarly, for Steve to share his dreams, he also has to feel safe that I will listen, ask questions and encourage him.

When we share our dreams, we are opening our hearts. Because of this, it is important when one spouse shares a dream that the other doesn't knock it down with all the reasons why "that will never happen." I have known some marriages that no longer share deep thoughts or dreams. When I dug deeper with them, I discovered that every creative idea or dream was met with ten reasons why it couldn't happen. Eventually, opening up about those dreams simply ended.

Remember that dreaming doesn't mean "the dream" has to happen. It is not a bucket list. Instead, dreaming is opening up about possibilities, opportunities, and visions.

S teve—As I write this, I am sitting in a condo that a dear friend has provided to Pam and me at no charge. The condo is on Longboat Key, Florida, right on the beach overlooking the Gulf Coast. At this moment, I am looking out the sliding glass doors at the shimmering blue ocean. The sun is lowering on the horizon. It's late afternoon. The water is glistening like diamonds. It is a breathtaking sight!

As if it can't get any better, in a few hours the sun will set and the sky will explode into a million shades of orange, red, blue and grey. God's handiwork is resplendent beyond words in this place!

Looking back on four decades of ministry, I cannot begin to count the number of marriages I have performed. Like the sunsets on Longboat Key, each one had its own special beauty. All of those marriages were launched with bucket loads of hopes and dreams. I have yet to see a bride who was not gorgeous. But, sadly, too many times I have watched those same marriages decay and crumble. The reasons are many and often complex. But I've seen one constant—once a couple stops dreaming together, it becomes increasingly hard to weather the other storms they may be navigating.

Actress Celeste Holm said this: "We live by encouragement and die without it—slowly, sadly, angrily." I would paraphrase like this regarding marriage: "Marriages live by dreams and die without them—slowly, sadly and often angrily."

So keep dreaming together—because it's another vital secret to a sizzling marriage!

As we wrap up, Pam and I would like to pray for you...

If you are not yet married, we pray that this book might give you a blueprint to architect your future marriage.

If you are unhappily married, we pray that this book might give you insights to redirect your course into green pastures and calm waters.

If you are happily married, we pray that this book hones your strengths and leads to even more passionate love-making than ever.

If you were once married and have lost hope, we pray that this book would ignite a new vision for a future marriage that would become all we've written about and more.

Discussion Questions

Chapter One - Secret #1
Put Christ First

1. Describe to your spouse a time when you felt especially close to God. What were the circumstances?

_____

_____

_____

_____

_____

How did you feel?

_____

_____

_____

_____

_____

How long ago did it take place?

_____

_____

2.   Share with your spouse one or two things that may be getting in the way for you to have a Christ-centered personal life and a Christ-centered marriage.

_____

_____

_____

_____

_____

Talk about what adjustments each of you would be willing to make to move toward a more Christ-centered life.

3.   If you practiced more consistently one spiritual habit (such as personal Bible study, prayer, church attendance, generosity, etc.), how might it help your spiritual growth?

_____

_____

_____

_____

Describe to your spouse what it would take for you to begin doing that spiritual habit more consistently.

_____

_____

_____

_____

_____

4. When you think about a "marriage that sizzles," what comes to mind?

_____

_____

_____

_____

As a couple, write down a vision statement in one sentence describing how you see your marriage in five years.

_____

_____

_____

_____

5.   Hold hands as a couple, close your eyes and pray out loud for each other. We know this may feel awkward for some at first. Prayer is simply talking to God. Use your own words and ask God to bless your spouse. Ask God to help you become all that he wants you to become. Pray that God gives you a marriage that sizzles!

Chapter Two - Secret #2
Become Best Friends

1. Describe to your spouse your "best friend" growing up.

_____

_____

_____

_____

_____

Who was it?

_____

Why did you get along so well?

_____

_____

_____

_____

_____

2. Would you say that you are currently "best friends" with your spouse?

_____

Why or why not?

_____

_____

_____

_____

_____

What would it take to become "best friends" together?

_____

_____

_____

_____

_____

3. Share with your spouse what you enjoy doing with him or her. List 5 or 10 things you enjoy doing together most.

_____

_____

_____

_____

_____

4. Do you have friends as a couple?

_____

_____

_____

_____

Who are they?

_____

_____

_____

How do they help you in your marriage?

_____

_____

_____

_____

_____

Do they hinder your marriage in any way?

_____

_____

_____

_____

_____

5. Describe what personal interest you have that you might be willing to curtail to have more time and energy to develop common interests together as a couple.

_____

_____

_____

_____

_____

Chapter Three - Secret #3
Selflessly Serve Each Other

1. What does the word "selfless" suggest to you?

_____

_____

_____

_____

_____

Does it evoke negative feelings or positive?

_____

_____

_____

_____

_____

What is the most selfless act you have ever personally experienced?

_____

_____

_____

_____

_____

Why was it selfless?

_____

_____

_____

_____

2. Describe in your own words what it means to live "in the way of Christ."

_____

_____

_____

_____

_____

Has there ever been a time when you felt that you lived "in the way of Christ?"

_____

_____

_____

_____

_____

When was it?

_____

_____

_____

_____

Describe how you felt.

_____

_____

_____

_____

3.   Tell your spouse something they do that you view as selfless.

_____

_____

_____

_____

_____

Have your spouse share something that you do that they view as selfless.

_____

_____

_____

_____

_____

4.   Look through the lists of suggestions for husbands and wives to become more selfless in marriage. From Steve's list, have the wife pick one suggestion she would like her husband to do.

_____

_____

_____

_____

From Pam's list, have the husband pick one suggestion he would like his wife to do.

_____

_____

_____

_____

_____

5.   Husband—Pray the husband's prayer as you hold your wife closely in your arms.

_____

_____

_____

_____

_____

Wife—Pray the wife's prayer as you hold your husband closely in your arms. (For those that want extra credit you can pray naked!)

_____

_____

_____

_____

_____

Chapter Four - Secret #4
Forgive and Move Forward

1. If you are a Christ follower, describe how you felt when you first experienced God's forgiveness.

_____

_____

_____

_____

_____

What made it so meaningful to you?

_____

_____

_____

_____

If you are not yet a Christ follower, would you consider asking the Lord to forgive you?

_____

This is done through a simple prayer asking for God's forgiveness. There is no special formula. Use your own words and ask the Lord to forgive you and come into your life.

2.   Is there anything for which you need to ask your spouse's forgiveness?

_____

_____

_____

_____

_____

Take your time on this. If you are genuinely repentant, be open and honest with each other. While looking into each other's eyes, ask for forgiveness.

3. Is there anything you are still holding against your spouse that needs to be released?

_____

_____

_____

_____

_____

The secret in this chapter is to forgive and move forward. We can't move forward until we release. If you are still holding onto something, tell your spouse what it is and talk together about steps you can take to put it behind you.

Chapter Five - Secret #5
Enjoy Lingering Conversations

1. If it seems intimidating to have a "lingering conversation," describe for your spouse why that is.

_____

_____

_____

_____

_____

Describe the feelings that are evoked in you when you think about having an open-ended, soul-baring conversation with your spouse.

_____

_____

_____

_____

_____

2. In your understanding, what is a "lingering conversation?"

_____

_____

_____

_____

Have you ever had one with your spouse? How about with someone else?

_____

_____

_____

_____

3. Time alone as a married couple is essential to have a "lingering conversation." Talk to each other about the last time you were alone for a sufficient amount of time to have a "lingering conversation."

_____

_____

_____

_____

How long ago was it?

_____

_____

_____

_____

What steps could you take to carve out more time alone together?

_____

_____

_____

_____

_____

4.   When was the last time each of you gave the benefit of the doubt to each other?

_____

_____

_____

_____

_____

Was it easy or was it hard? Why?

_____

_____

_____

_____

_____

5.   Decide which spouse will research getting a resource with insightful questions for married couples. Plan a date when you can be alone together for several hours to ask each other the most intriguing questions in the resource you have chosen.

Chapter Six - Secret #6
Intentionally Invest In Your Marriage

1.   Have you ever intentionally done something to create a memory as a married couple?

_____

_____

_____

_____

_____

If so, when was it?

_____

_____

_____

_____

How did it make you feel?

_____

_____

_____

_____

_____

2.   Have both husband and wife describe to each other, in their own words, what it might mean to more intentionally invest in your marriage.

_____

_____

_____

_____

_____

3.   Have both husband and wife share one "off-the-charts" experience that each of you dreams about doing together as a couple.

_____

_____

_____

_____

_____

What would it take to actually do it?

_____

_____

_____

_____

_____

4.   What do you both need to say "no" to in order
to allocate more time and resources to invest in your
marriage?

_____

_____

_____

_____

_____

Chapter Seven - Secret #7
Pray Naked

1. If you have never prayed naked as a married couple, Pam and I encourage you to try this at the next opportune moment. For some people, praying out loud is awkward. But remember that God is not impressed by our eloquence. He simply wants us to communicate with him.

So hold each other closely and share with God whatever is on your heart.

At the very least, thank God for your spouse and pray blessings on each other as you embrace.

2. Discuss together what it means to become spiritually united as a couple. Is there anything hindering this in your relationship?

_____

_____

_____

_____

_____

3. Discuss together what it means to become emotionally united as a married couple.

_____

_____

_____

_____

_____

Does anything come to mind that might help your emotional oneness to deepen? Share those thoughts and feelings with each other.

_____

_____

_____

4. What is one daily rhythm that you both agree would help your spiritual or emotional oneness as a married couple?

_____

_____

_____

_____

_____

What is stopping you from beginning this new rhythm?

_____

_____

_____

_____

_____

Chapter Eight - Secret #8
Have Sex Often

1. Look back over Pam and Steve's sex advice. What things caught your attention?

Talk about those as a couple. Share as openly as you can with each other.

2.   On a scale of 1-10 (with 10 being the highest), how would each of you rate your communication about your sexual relationship?

_____

_____

_____

_____

_____

If you are on the lower end of the scale, what could you do to improve this?

_____

_____

_____

_____

3.   Have both husband and wife share their top five love-making memories as a married couple.

_____

_____

_____

_____

Describe why each specific memory is special to you.

_____

_____

_____

_____

_____

4.   While looking each other in the eyes and holding hands, tell your spouse one thing that you especially enjoy about your sexual relationship.

_____

_____

_____

_____

_____

5.   Now, still holding hands and looking into each other's eyes, share one thing you would like to change.

_____

_____

_____

_____

_____

Chapter Nine - Secret #9
Release Disappointments

1. What is the greatest disappointment you have experienced personally, and as a married couple?

_____

_____

_____

_____

_____

In what way does it still impact you?

_____

_____

_____

_____

2.   Which of the steps to release disappointments mentioned by Steve and Pam were most helpful to you?

_____

_____

_____

_____

_____

3.   Share with each other what you have done to put disappointments behind you.

_____

_____

_____

_____

_____

4.   In what ways might disappointment still affect your marriage relationship?

_____

_____

_____

_____

_____

Does one disappointment drag you down more than the others? Which one and why?

_____

_____

_____

_____

_____

5.   Turn your hands upward and look into each other's eyes. Pray out loud a prayer of surrender, offering to God any disappointment that may you still be holding onto.

_____

_____

_____

_____

_____

Chapter Ten - Secret #10
Keep Dreaming Together

1.   On a scale of 1-10 (with 10 being the highest), rate the frequency and passion of the dreams you have as a married couple.

_____

_____

_____

_____

_____

2.   Share with each other five dreams that each of you have as a married couple in the next five years.

_____

_____

_____

_____

_____

3. Discuss what it would take for your marriage to become more "dream friendly."

_____

_____

_____

_____

4. The next opportunity you have as a couple, pray naked together about the dreams you have for your marriage.

_____

_____

_____

_____

Take your time. Enjoy the journey!

Notes

Chapter Three - Secret #3

Selflessly Serve Each Other

1. "Love shouldn't be this hard…"

Page 72, The Meaning of Marriage: Facing the Complexities of Commitment with the Wisdom of God, Timothy Keller with Kathy Keller, Riverhead Books, New York, New York, 2011.

2. Quoting scholar John White, Jr, "The earlier ideal of marriage…."

Page 20, The Meaning of Marriage: Facing the Complexities of Commitment with the Wisdom of God, Timothy Keller with Kathy Keller, Riverhead Books, New York, New York, 2011.

Chapter Four - Secret #4
Forgive and Move Forward

1. "The world has yet to see...."
Dwight L. Moody quotes in Christian Quotes.info.

Chapter Six - Secret #6
Intentionally Invest In Your Marriage

1. The Five Love Languages: How to Express Heartfelt Commitment to Your Mate, Gary Chapman, Northfield Publishing, Chicago, IL, 1995.

2. "I've watched the speed which we live...."
Page 9, Little House on the Freeway: Help for the Hurried Home, Tim Kimmel, Multnomah Books, Colorado Springs, CO, 2008.

Chapter Seven - Secret #7
Pray Naked

1. "Sweethearts who have been wise enough..."
Page 106, Letters by a Modern Mystic, Frank Laubach, Purposeful Design Publications, Colorado Springs, CO, 2007.

2. "It is like being suddenly..."

Page 191, Classics of Faith and Devotion, A Life of Prayer, Faith and Passion for God Alone. Edited by James M. Houston, Bethany House Publishers, Ada, MI, 1983.

Chapter Eight - Secret #8
Have Sex Often

1. "Men want women to know that they want more sex..."

Page 111, For Women Only, Shaunti Feldhahn, Multnomah Books, Colorado Springs, CO, 2004.

2. "Has your husband ever come up behind you..."

Page 136-137, Sheet Music: Uncovering the Secrets of Sexual Intimacy in Marriage, Kevin Leman, Tyndale House Publishers, Carol Stream, IL, 2008.

3. "Many husbands get more satisfaction from bringing their wives to orgasm..."

Page 109, Sheet Music: Uncovering the Secrets of Sexual Intimacy in Marriage, Kevin Leman, Tyndale House Publishers, Carol Stream, IL, 2008.

Chapter Ten - Secret #10
Keep Dreaming Together

1. "The third adulthood..."

Generational IQ: Christianity isn't dying, millennials aren't the problem, and the future is bright, Haydn Shaw with Ginger Kolbada, Tyndale House Publishers, Carol Stream, IL, 2015.

Information

For information about Steve and Pam Bond, or to book them for speaking engagements, please visit: www.livingwellministries.biz

Additional Contact:

Living Well Ministries LLC
Post Office Box 50177
Sparks, NV 89435